AF600661

THE CATHOLIC UNIVERSITY OF AMERICA
CANON LAW STUDIES
Number 65

SIMONY

AN HISTORICAL SYNOPSIS AND COMMENTARY

A DISSERTATION

Submitted to the Faculty of Canon Law of the Catholic University of America in Partial Fulfillment of the Requirements for the Degree of

DOCTOR OF CANON LAW

BY

REV. RAYMOND A. RYDER, A.B., J.C.L.
Priest of the Archdiocese of Philadelphia

THE CATHOLIC UNIVERSITY OF AMERICA
WASHINGTON, D. C.
1931

Nihil Obstat

VALENTINUS SCHAAF, O.F.M., J.C.D.
Censor Deputatus

WASHINGTONII, D. C., DIE III MARTII, 1931

Imprimatur

✠DIONYSIUS CARDINALIS DOUGHERTY
Archiepiscopus Philadelphiensis

PHILADELPHIAE, DIE III MARTII, 1931

WASHINGTON TYPOGRAPHERS, INC.
WASHINGTON, D. C.

TO MY MOTHER

FOREWORD

The very word *simony* has an archaic ring. It suggests nothing modern and hence there is a tendency to relegate the abuse to former ages and to view the legislation surrounding it as something historical. But the avaricious, like the poor, we have always with us. Commentators on the Code of Canon Law, as a rule, devote but little space to the consideration of the vice, many contenting themselves with a mere paraphrase of the canons. No one has undertaken a study of the question in English. It was the desire to present a concise analysis of the attitude of the Church at the present time, as well as a keen interest in the subject, which prompted the choice of the topic of this dissertation.

A word must be said concerning the historical discussion of the laws preceding the Code. The present legislation contains little which is new. Some of the prohibitions and sanctions can be traced back to the earliest ages of the Church. To be understood, they must be examined under the circumstances which surrounded their enactment. To take a canon from its historical environment, is to divorce a text from its context. On the other hand, one must not expect to find within the narrow confines of a single chapter, a detailed and critical history to which not even volumes could do justice.

In treating of the definition of simony, as well as its various divisions, it was thought expedient to invade the field of Moral Theology, and to dwell upon some things which are foreign to the scope of Canon Law. It was the desire to bring out in still bolder relief the real nature of the vice, that prompted the effort to trace the simoniacal act from its very inception in the mind. Some attention has been given, therefore, to matters which pertain to the internal forum, but the understanding of which makes for a clearer view of the canonical aspects of simony. In the historical survey, it was deemed expedient to pass over some things which might occupy the attention of a student of ecclesiastical history, but which would shed little light upon the present laws. It is sincerely hoped that any such digressions or omissions will prove a help rather than a hindrance.

The writer takes this occasion to express his gratitude to the Faculty of Canon Law for their interest and assistance, to Rev. Nicholas A. Weber, S. M., S. T. D., for his many valuable suggestions, and to all those who have cooperated in the preparation of this study.

TABLE OF CONTENTS

PART I

HISTORICAL DEVELOPMENT

CHAPTER I

LEGISLATION BEFORE THE CODE

Article I.—Pre-christian Era

Though the chief concern of the present work should be to consider the attitude of the Church toward simony, it might not be without profit to draw aside the veil for a momentary glance at the history of the epochs which were closed with the coming of Christ. Theologians[1] usually divide the history of the world into four parts. The first, they term *The State of Innocence,* which lasted from the creation to the expulsion of Adam and Eve from the garden of Paradise. The second period, extending from the Fall to the promulgation of the Mosaic law for the Jews, and for the Gentiles, to the coming of Christ, they call *The State of the Law of Nature,* because during that time, men were guided not by written tables of law, but by the law which was graven in their hearts. For the Jews, a third epoch began with the promulgation of the *Law of Moses.* Lastly came the Christian era, or the period of the *Law of the New Testament.*

Concerning the possibility of simony in the *State of the Law of Nature,*[2] there should be no difficulty. There was certainly a sufficiency of spiritual objects which might tempt the avarice of men. Since simony is forbidden by the natural law, there can be no doubt that the prohibition of this vice existed in the earliest times, even as it does today. But no positive precept can be found in this period.[3]

What Weber[4] says of the Church can be applied very readily to the Mosaic dispensation. "Ruled by men, and dealing with

[1] Tanquerey, *Synopsis Theologiae Dogmaticae,* III, n. 239.

[2] Since the *State of Innocence* was of such short duration, and concerned only two persons, it may be passed over in silence.

[3] Gibalinus, *De Simonia,* q. 6, c. 1; Pichler, *Jus Canonicum,* lib. V, tit. III, n. 2.

[4] *History of Simony,* p. 26.

men, the Church had ever the source of simony within herself. Ambition and the love of wealth and ease, are to be met with in every human heart, and are bound to manifest themselves in any great and durable human organization, however lofty its principles and end.'' Nevertheless, one of the greatest sources of simony in the New Testament, had been removed from the Mosaic period. The sacred ministry was transmitted in hereditary succession. Care of the sanctuary, and incidentally the collection of any revenues connected with such duties, devolved upon the sons of Aaron and Levi.[5] Authors[6] quote numerous examples of the crime in the books of the Old Testament,[7] seeing in the narration by the sacred writers of the punishments therein inflicted, a purpose of filling the people with a horror of this vice. Gibalinus[8] considers the words of the prophets positive precepts forbidding traffic in holy things.

Article II.—The Early Church

Whilst Israel was under the dominion of foreigners and pagans, ambitious Jews availed themselves of the opportunity to purchase the office of priesthood from them. Hence we find simoniacal traffic flourishing at the very beginning of the Christian era. Caiphas, the high priest at the time of the death of Christ, had purchased his pontifical office from Herod.[9] In the Christian Church, the first instance of simony seems to have been the betrayal of the Master by Judas.[10] ''But the crime bore such an exceptional and repulsive character; its consequences were so tragic and appalling, that the apparently simoniacal feature of the act became secondary in men's minds

[5] Exodus, XXVIII, 1, XXIX, 44, XL, 13; Leviticus, VIII; Numbers, III.

[6] Thomassinus, *Vetus et Nova Disciplina,* VII, c. 55, n. 1; Ferraris, *Biblioth.,* v. *Simonia,* art. I, n. 7.

[7] Exodus, XXII, 8; Numbers, XXII, 7, 17, 37; IV Kings, V, 20; Micheas, III, 11.

[8] *De Simonia,* q. 6, c. 1.

[9] Flavius Josephus, *Antiquitatum Judaicarum,* lib. XVIII, c. 2, n. 3; Thomassinus, *Vetus et Nova Disciplina,* VII, c. 55, n. 2; Jerome, *Commentarium in Matt.,* c. 26 (MPL, 26, 201).

[10] Leinz, *Die Simonie,* p. 1.

and rightly received but scant mention in history."[11] Yet it is the very character of the crime which leads Gibalinus[12] to deny that Judas was guilty of simony. Such a transaction, he admits, contains a sacrilege of the most reprehensible kind, which surpasses every sin of simony, bearing only an analogical relation to it.

Simony takes its name from Simon Magus, whose attempt to buy the power of the Holy Ghost evoked condemnation from St. Peter.[13] Much of the early Christian literature concerning Simon is apocryphal, but from some of the genuine writings, it is possible to sketch a fairly accurate account of this much discussed character. He was born at Gitton, in Samaria. Of his early life, practically nothing is known. From the Acts of the Apostles, one can gather that he had been displaying his power for some time in Samaria, when Philip the deacon came there to preach, and naturally his magic had secured for him an extensive following. The miracles performed by Philip in proof of the new doctrine greatly weakened Simon's influence with the people. He became desirous of possessing this new power, not only to regain his lost prestige, but also because he saw in it a source of immense revenue.[14] In the pseudo-Clementine literature of the third century, Simon Magus is represented as the arch-heretic with whom Peter contended in defense of the true faith.[15] Ebionite hostility to the Apostle Paul saw in these passages a covert attack upon Paul under the cloak of Simon. This led many authors to deny the existence of such a character as Simon Magus. In their opinion, the

[11] Weber, *History of Simony*, p. 17.

[12] *De Simonia*, q. 6, c. 16; cf. Suarez, *Opera Omnia*, tom. XIII, lib. IV, c. 9, n. 4.

[13] Acts, VIII, 18-21.

[14] Ireneus, *Adversus Haereses*, lib. I, c. 23, (*MPG*, 7, 670-673); lib. II, c. 9, n. 2, (*MPG*, 7, 739); lib. II, c. 31, (*MPG*, 7, 823); Justin Martyr, *Apologia*, I, c. 26, (*MPG*, 6, 367); I, c. 56, (*MPG*, 6, 414); Tertullian, *De Anima*, c. 34, (*MPL*, 2, 708); McGiffert, *History of Christianity*, p. 99; Funk, *Manual of Church History*, I, 78; Bigg, *Origins of Christianity*, pp. 43, 130; Edmundson, *Church in Rome*, pp. 60-65; de Pressense, *Early Years*, pp. 66, 68, 71, 73, 318, 319, 321; Burke, *Characteristics of the Early Church*, p. 93.

[15] McGiffert, *History of Christianity*, p. 100, note 1.

account of the Acts would then have to be disregarded as entirely unhistorical. It is now generally recognized that this procedure is unwarranted.

Simony was an offence nearly excluded by the nature of the case from the first three centuries of Church History. Persecutions foretold by Christ were rending the Church asunder; preferment conveyed but little worldly power or distinction; it involved a more direct exposure to attack. Martyrdom was, as it were, annexed to every bishopric, and the first persons to be sought out by the agents of the persecutors, were the rulers of the Church. Hence, few persons were likely to aspire to ecclesiastical dignities from other than the holiest motives; there was no great danger from ambitious spirits, nor any occasion to make laws against simoniacal promotions.[16] Tertullian noted the marked contrast between pagan and Christian religions.[17] The rulers of the Christian church secured their honors by election, not purchase; nor was a price set upon anything; though there were boxes for offerings, no money was exacted from the people.

In the year 268, the Council of Antioch condemned Paul of Samosata, on the grounds that he had freely and extensively used his spiritual office to enrich himself.[18] The incident of the condemnation of Paul was significant of the attitude of the Church, and might be considered as a foreshadowing of the general legislation which was soon to follow. One can see in it the beginning of the evolution, the stamping out of the vice in particular instances, which was the forerunner of the prohibition later made for the entire Church.

It is evident that the comparative peace and quiet of the Constantinian era had produced considerable secularity in the Church. With the recognition of Christianity by the State, ecclesiastical dignities were elevated to a high rank and soon became objects of secular ambition. Then, too, the means of

[16] Bingham, *Antiquities*, I, 483; Fleury-Newman, *Ecclesiastical History*, III, 17; Bright, *Notes on the First Four General Councils*, p. 127.

[17] *Apologia*, XXXIX, (*MPL*, 1, 469).

[18] Eusebius, *Historia Ecclesiastica*, VII, c. 30 (*MPG*, 20, 711).

support for the clergy adopted in those early days gave rise to many abuses.

The earliest legislation against simony comes from the Council of Elvira in Spain, about the year 300.[19] In the earlier days, donations were made by catechumens at the time of Baptism. That these donations were gratuitous is evident from the purity of the existing discipline and the fact that they were put into the *gazophylacium*.[20] As time passed, the free donations did not increase in proportion to the needs of the Church and its ministers, and the custom of exacting a fee for the administration of Baptism was introduced. The Council of Elvira decreed the abolition of the custom of catechumens' placing an offering in the shell which was used in the administration of Baptism. The words of the Council would lead us to believe that the Spanish donations were made willingly, but because of the appearances of simony, it was deemed advisable to condemn the practice.[21]

Some see in the 15th and 16th canons of the Council of Nicea[22] (325) a direct attack upon an abuse, which, while not simoniacal in itself, at least might open the way to simony. Episcopal vacancies were very frequently occasions for intrigue in favor of this or that prelate who would regard translation as a promotion.[23] The Council of Nicea[24] declared that such agreements

[19] C. 48—Mansi, I, 13; Hefele, *Conciliengeschichte*, I, 177. This has been incorporated in the Corpus Juris Canonici, c. 104, C. I, q. 1.

[20] The *gazophylacium* was a receptacle for free donations. Cf. Keller, *Mass Stipends*, p. 18.

[21] "Whence we may conclude, that if the people might not offer, the priest might not exact nor demand anything for the administration of Baptism."—Bingham, *Antiquities*, II, 76.

[22] Mansi, II, 674-675.

[23] The Sardican Council in its very first canon, remarked with a touch of sarcasm that no bishop had yet been found to aim at being transferred from a greater see to a lesser one. It also inferred that the pernicious abuse was indicative of a passionate eagerness for more money, or an arrogant craving for more power. Cf. Bright, *Notes*, p. 49.

[24] Ghilardi (*Epitome Canonum*, II, 489) alleges the 49th canon of Nicea (Arabic Collection) as directly forbidding under pain of deposition, the acceptance of money for ordination. It is generally agreed, however, that the Arabic Collection is not authentic, and that the only genuine canons are the twenty usually attributed to this Council. Cf. Hefele, *Conciliengeschichte*, I, 367.

would be null and void, and the person transferred must be restored to the Church from which he came.[25]

Athanasius[26] accuses the Arians of sending out bishops as if from a market on receipt of gold. Eighteen years later, the Fathers of Sardica, (343)[27] vigorously condemned the acquisition of bishoprics by bribing the people to demand certain candidates. Osius, a bishop, arose in the Council and proposed that if a person declared that he had received testimonial letters,[28] it would be manifest that he had bribed the people to procure his election. Such practices should be condemned and the offenders deprived of even lay communion. The Council had plainly in mind the Arians and their adherents who, as soon as they had won over a small party in a town, sought to press into the bishoprics.[29]

One of the earliest and most comprehensive pieces of legislation against simoniacal traffic was enacted at the council of Chalcedon,[30] in the year 451. Canon 2 covers almost every possible case of purchasing orders, not only extending to major and minor orders, but also to such appointments which did not

---

[25] However, the 14th Apostolic Canon should not be overlooked. This allowed the transfer of bishops when some greater benefit could be secured to the people of the place whither the prelate would be transferred. Thus, if a bishop of an obscure town had the gift of eloquence which would tell powerfully upon the society of a metropolis, this would be sufficient reason for such a transfer. What the Council meant to strike at was obviously the translation associated with worldly motives, tending to scandalous discord. Cf. Bright, *Notes*, p. 49.

[26] *Historia Arian.*, LXXIII, (*MPG*, 25, 782).

[27] C. 1, 2,—Mansi, III, 7.

[28] Weber (*History*, p. 62) adds "from the more important see."

[29] The addition of the Latin text, "*qui sinceram fidem non habent,*" is found in Dionysius Exiguus and in the Prisca, as well as in Isadore, and its meaning is this. In a town, some few, *especially those who had not the true faith,* can easily be bribed to demand this or that person as their bishop. In the Corpus Juris Canonici, it has a further addition, "*nisi hoc poenituerit,*" i.e., such a one shall not on his deathbed, receive even lay communion, unless he has repented of his fault. Raymond of Pennaforte, in collecting the Decretals, probably added this to conform the canon to the later practice in this respect. Cf. c. 2, X *de electione,* I, 6; Hefele, *Conciliengeschichte,* I, 559; Bright, *Notes,* p. 127.

[30] C. 8, C. I, q. 1; Hefele, *Conciliengeschichte,* II, 506.

require ordination. Bishops were forbidden to ordain for money, other bishops, priests, deacons, or in fact any cleric. They were not permitted to accept money for the nomination of stewards, advocates, porters, or any other person on the roll of the Church. Upon conviction, the penalties were deposition for the offending bishop and suspension for the ordained. Intermediaries or accomplices were included in these penalties. Clerics who acted in this capacity were deposed, and laics were anathematized. Monks were assimilated to laymen in this matter.

It seems that the decree of this council was soon disregarded, for seven years afterward, at a synod held at Constantinople[31] under Gennadius I (459-460), the canon was again brought up. The assembled Bishops renewed the second canon of Chalcedon, adding also that in the case of simoniacal ordinations, it was doubtful whether grace was conferred. A curious point in this legislation is the fact that it mattered little whether the accused were convicted or not. A circular letter issued at the synod expressly declared, that the penalties of excommunication and deposition would be inflicted upon the guilty party, even though he were not convicted.[32]

At this point may be mentioned the Apostolic Canons which treat of the bartering of offices. The date of the composition of these canons has been much disputed.[33] It should be sufficient to note that Dionysius Exiguus found them in existence when he made his Latin translation of the canons about the year 500.[34] Canon 30[35] threatens with deposition and excommunication both the one who simoniacally conferred orders and the one who received them. Only the major orders are enumerated, but since the canon forbids the selling of the ἀξίως, it is at least

[31] Hefele, *Conciliengeschichte*, II, 584.

[32] Weber (*History of Simony*, p. 71) inclines toward the interpretation that the judges in the case have certain knowledge but no legal proofs, and pronounce deposition upon their own convictions.

[33] *Dictionnaire d'archeol. Chret. et de Liturg.*, v. canons apostoliques, t. II, par. II, pp. 1910-1950; Vermeersch-Creusen, *Epitome*, I, n. 12; Cocchi, *Commentarium*, I, n. 23; Funk, *Die Apostolischen Konstitutionen* (Rottenburg, 1891), 187-191.

[34] Weber, *History of Simony*, p. 66.

[35] Hefele, *Conciliengeschichte*, I, 809.

insinuated that not only the order and the sacrament are meant, but also the office or benefice.[36] In the thirty-first canon it is forbidden for bishops to make use of the secular power in securing office, and the enormity of the crime can be seen in the fact that both degradation and excommunication are inflicted on the offenders.

The historical study of the attitude of the early Church consists merely in a consideration of the measures adopted in particular cases, when it became necessary to suppress abuses. Yet, it is in this early period that the nucleus is to be found of the legislation which, in later years, was to assume gigantic proportions. The canons of Elvira and Chalcedon have been reechoed even in the latest revision of the law, and they form the foundation upon which the Church has built her bulwark against those whose avarice is carried into the sanctuary.

Article III.—From the Sixth to the Twelfth Century

The Church came forth from the catacombs, when Christianity had been recognized by the State. Some years after the death of Constantine, persecution again broke out, though its fury was of somewhat lesser intensity than the earlier assaults. The covert attacks of Julian the Apostate and the more open warfare of Valens, did much to keep the crime of simony from becoming more widespread. The repeated invasions of the barbarians so occupied men with the defense of their own lives, that they had little time to think of securing ecclesiastical positions. Withal, the evil was not entirely suppressed, even for a time, as is evident from the legislation of these early centuries.

§ 1. *The Church in Italy*

The election of Pope Symmachus had been attended with much disorder and corruption. Accordingly one of his first pontifical acts was to summon a synod at Rome, to provide against a similar occurrence at future elections. Although the word *simony* is avoided, one can readily see that the Pope's intention was to forestall any illicit negotiations in the choice

[36] Thomassinus, *Vetus et Nova Disciplina*, VII, c. 49, n. 1.

of a Pontiff. Deprivation of dignity and of communion were threatened if anyone should bind himself to vote for a certain candidate during the lifetime of the Pope, or should make any attempts to secure the papacy before the See became vacant.[37] Perhaps the most curious point in this legislation is the special provision made in favor of those who, even though implicated in the negotiations, would bring to the notice of the proper authorities the necessary information concerning the intrigue. Such persons would not only escape the prescribed penalties, but would receive a suitable reward.[38]

The laws enacted against charging or even accepting money for ordinations had been explicit. Men, then, began to cast about for some excuse whereby they could exact payment from candidates for orders, and yet evade the penalties attached to such abuses. The conferring of the pallium, the consecration of bishops and especially the documents connected with the conferring of such things, seemed to present a solution to the problem.[39] Five years after his election, Gregory the Great[40]

---

[37] C. 1, 2—Hefele, *Conciliengeschichte,* II, 625. One can see here reflected the same circumstances which occurred at the Council of Sardica, but where the latter sought degradation for the elected, the present synod aimed at venality among the electors.

[38] C. 4—Hefele, *loc. cit.*

[39] Gonzalez, *Commentarium Perpetuum,* lib. V, tit. III, c. 1.

[40] That Gregory the Great was the arch-enemy of simony is freely admitted. "It is his influence on the development of anti-simoniacal legislation that we wish to indicate here. Just as some of the decrees of his predecessors and of councils on this point were received into the 'Corpus Juris Canonici,' so likewise some of Gregory's utterances became and still remain ecclesiastical law. It is true that some of his prohibitions contained little that was new. The sale of ecclesiastical offices, especially bishoprics, had been frequently forbidden before him. The episcopal office had become a much coveted position at an early date, and restrictive legislation was the consequence. The ecclesiastical organization had not been modified to the extent of demanding in Gregory's time new laws prohibitive of simony, or any considerable extension of the old ones. Eccles astical patronage . . . had not yet received sufficient development to lead to grave abuses. Benefices had come into existence under the name of *Precariae,* but were still in the formative period of their history. The sale of sacramental graces other than ordination was not universally prevalent. Hence as regards the spiritual object of a simoniacal transaction, Gregory made

summoned a council at Rome to take action against these practices. Decrees were enacted forbidding the charging of money for any of these functions, upon any pretext whatsoever, not even for the *pastellum.*[41] In the decree, the office of "notary" is expressly mentioned, and from its close connection with the words "bishop" and "minister," Thomassinus argues that the office of notary was one of the minor orders of the Church at that time.[42] Definite as the prohibition was, it is indeed strange that it did nothing more than emphasize the theological guilt connected with simony. For the canon merely stated that violators of this law would incur guilt in the sight of God.[43]

A decree of Nicholas I[44] deserves attention for the fine distinctions which it made in the cases of simoniacal ordinations.[45] The Pontiff mentioned three classes of offenders, viz. those who purchased ordination from a bishop who himself had been simoniacally consecrated, those who purchased ordination from one who had been rightfully consecrated, and finally those who were rightfully ordained by a bishop who had paid for his own consecration. The first two classes were to be deprived of the office which they had secured by purchase, while the third class was permitted to retain their position if necessity demanded it.

---

no addition to the already existing legislation. There was one point, however, which either consciously or unconsciously was misinterpreted in Gregory's time, viz., the meaning of the expression 'present, reward, earthly price.' . . . It became imperative to take decisive action against these abuses, and Gregory permanently stated the full meaning of the earthly price given in exchange for something spiritual. . . . It was in one of his homilies (*Hom. in Evang.* i, iv, 4,—*MPL,* 76, 1091), that he gave the threefold division of the price into '*Munus ab obsequio, munus a manu, munus a lingua.*' . . . Subsequent ages have brought no addition to this interpretation of the temporal price."—Weber, *History of Simony,* pp. 196-199.

[41] Hefele (*Conciliengeschichte,* III, 58) renders this a "small repast, gratuity." Weber (*History of Simony,* p. 155) prefers "Seal," as yielding a more obvious meaning.

[42] *Vetus et Nova Disciplina,* VII, c. 62, n. 2.

[43] The Council did not forbid the acceptance of gratuitous offerings.

[44] Mansi, XV, 440.

[45] Schmalzgrueber (*Jus Ecclesiasticum Universum,* lib. V, tit. III, n. 102) attributes this decree to Nicholas II.

This decree, however, made no provision for the good or bad faith of the recipient of the Orders. Clement II pronounced the sentence of excommunication against those who *knowingly* received Orders from a simoniacal bishop and imposed upon them forty days of ecclesiastical penance.[46]

Nicholas II took a decisive step toward the purification of the papal election. In the Cardinal Bishops and secular clergy, together with religious minded laics, was vested the power to expel from the See of Peter any intruder and to put into his place one who, in their judgment, was worthy of the dignity. Should they be unable to hold such an election within the city, they had apostolic authority to assemble where they could and to proceed to elect a candidate who, besides being the most worthy, will give promise of being most useful to the Holy See. The Pope-elect would enjoy at once plenary power, in the same sense as if he had already been crowned, to govern and provide for the interests of the Church. By this decree all rights of future emperors to participate in the election were withdrawn.[47]

The Council of Rome in 1078 under Gregory VII went still farther in its effort to stamp out avarice among the clergy. Any bishop who accepted money in exchange for discreet silence when there was question of serious crimes by a priest, deacon or sub-deacon, incurred suspension.[48] The Council of Piacenza in 1095, under Urban II, took up the question of simony in Baptism and christian burials, forbidding priests to exact anything on such occasions.[49] The eleventh century was brought to a close by the Council of Rome in 1099 under Urban II. After ratifying the provisions of the Council of Piacenza, the fathers considered the status of children for whom parents had secured through money ecclesiastical benefices. Such persons were to resign all claims to their positions. However, permission was granted to them to live canonically in these places, nor were they to be

---

[46] Mansi, IX, 721. The same attitude was adopted by Nicholas II. Cf. c. 109, C. I, q. 1.

[47] Mansi, XIX, 899; Jaffé, *Regesta Pontif. Roman.*, 559; Alzog, *Universal Church History*, II, 329.

[48] C. 4—Mansi, XX, 509.

[49] C. 7—Mansi, XX, 962.

removed from the orders which they had received, if they were otherwise capable of holding them.[50] Those who had purchased for themselves ecclesiastical offices, after they had become of age, must be transferred to another church if possible. If they can not be transferred they may remain there, but they become irregular and can not be advanced to higher orders. If they had been ordained, before the simoniacal purchase, they might be permitted to retain their status, unless their church was of such a nature that they would remain in the position of superior. Primates, archbishops and bishops were expressly forbidden to exact, demand or even accept any recompense from those whom they had ordained.[51]

Here one can see the beginnings of the legislation on benefices which was to occupy the rulers of the Church during the succeeding centuries. And here, too, it is evident that while the Church insisted upon the unworthy purchaser's being deprived of what he sought to buy, nevertheless she gave to the culprit whatever advantage she could without yielding a principle.

§ 2. *The Church in France*

The opposition to simony in France was quite marked. The Council of Orleans, in 533, accepted as adequate proof of a candidate's unworthiness, his offer of money for a bishopric.[52] Excommunication was a further development of the law at the Council of Clermont.[53]

An evil which bade fair to become a real menace had taken root in France and was thriving upon the venality and unscrupulousness of secular rulers. Powerful monarchs saw in ecclesiastical positions sources of immense revenue and did not hesitate to make such appointments as would fill their own coffers. They went so far as to remove the rightful holders of such positions and also to make gifts of benefices to others upon their own authority.[54] In the year 813, numerous councils

[50] C. 5—Mansi, XX, 962.

[51] C. 17—Mansi, XX, 962.

[52] C. 3—Mansi, VIII, 836; Hefele, *Conciliengeschichte*, II, 755.

[53] 535, c. 2—Hefele, *loc. cit.*, 761.

[54] Gonzalez, *Commentarium Perpetuum*, lib. V, tit. III, c. 3, a.

in no uncertain terms stated that any priest who was intruded into a church through monetary influence was *ipso facto* deposed. The warning was given to both cleric and lay that a church was to be bestowed upon no one without the consent of the bishop.[55]

Custom had been alleged on various occasions as a means of evading the law and its penalties. Such an appeal had been made when some were accused of illicit exaction of money for Sacred Chrism and for candles etc. The second Council of Chalons, in 813, stated that it was just as illicit to exact money for those things as it was for the dedication of a church or the conferring of orders.[56] Apparently some of those in power had accepted bribes to secure ordination for a candidate without the proper procedure or documents. The 16th canon of the Council of Nantes (895) forbade such practices, declaring the orders invalid and deposing the mediator if a cleric, and anathematizing him if a layman or monk.[57] It was absolutely forbidden to charge a fee for burials, Baptism, the Eucharist, or the visitation of the sick.[58]

§ 3. *The Church in Spain*

The major portion of the legislation in France and Italy was directed against venality in the matter of ordination. The Spanish Councils, on the other hand, attacked for the most part the simoniacal administration of the sacraments. One can notice immediately the severity of the Spanish discipline in this matter and such an attitude can only bespeak the great love of the Spanish people for the purity of religion. The Council of Elvira had forbidden even voluntary offerings at the time of Baptism because they presented the appearance of simony. But outside forces seem to have militated against the strict observance of the law,[59] and in the sixth century there was a modification of the early discipline. The Council of Braga

[55] Council of Tours, III, c. 15—Mansi, XIV, 85; Council of Rheims, II, c. 21—Mansi, XIV, 79; Council of Chalons, II, c. 42—Mansi, XIV, 102.

[56] Mansi, XIV, 97.

[57] Mansi, XVIII, 168.

[58] Council of Rheims, II, (1049), c. 2, 5—Mansi, XIX, 742-743.

[59] Devoti, *Institutiones,* II, lib. V, tit. IX, n. 7, 1°.

(572) while tolerating voluntary offerings forbade anything like an agreement or pledge to be exacted from the poor who were not able to offer anything.[60] Many of the poor people had been kept from presenting their children for Baptism because they had not sufficient money to satisfy the demands of the clergy. The Fathers did not hesitate to place the blame upon the men responsible for such conduct on the part of the parents, where the child died without Baptism.

The eleventh synod of Toledo (675) sought to eradicate with one bold stroke all venality from the administration of the sacraments. Payment was absolutely forbidden for Baptism, Confirmation and Orders. Bishops who tolerated a contrary custom were to incur excommunication for two months. Should the crime be committed without the bishop's knowledge, the penalties were to be incurred by the culprit alone. It is curious indeed that the degree of the punishment seems to have been in inverse proportion to the dignity of the delinquent. A priest was excommunicated for three months, a deacon for four, subdeacons and inferior clerics were not only excommunicated for an indefinite time, but were also to receive appropriate corporal punishment. At his consecration every bishop must swear that he did not and will not give money to anyone for his office.[61] With reference to fees for the administration of Baptism, the version of the canon given in Mansi would exclude even voluntary offerings. Thomassinus,[62] however, prefers a different reading, in which the word *nisi* is inserted before the expression *voluntarie oblata,* thus making exception for volun-

[60] C. 7—Mansi, IX, 893. Some editions of Gratian allege a canon of the 3rd or 4th Council of Carthage to the same purpose. There is no such canon to be found in any African Council. Cf. Bingham, *Antiquities,* II, 77.

[61] C. 8, 9—Mansi, XI, 142. Canon 9 contains a clause which seems out of harmony with the spirit of the law. It provides that if anyone is discovered to be a simonist, he is to be excommunicated. But if he does penance in exile for two years, he may not only be readmitted to communion, but he may again *be restored to his office.* Compare this with canon 3 of the tenth synod of Toledo, (653), (Mansi, XI, 34), which inflicted perpetual seclusion in a monastery for the purchase of orders.

[62] *Vetus et Nova Disciplina,* VII, c. 69, n. 2.

tary offerings. He bases his conclusion upon the change from the discipline of Elvira to that of Braga, and appeals to the existing customs to prove that spontaneous offerings were not forbidden by the law. The third council of Braga (675) permitted the accepting of voluntary offerings for the consecration of churches, but was quite definite in its prohibition of demanding a fee.[63] It also recalled a practice similar to that condemned by St. Basil,[64] where promises of money made before ordination were received after the ceremonies. Both donor and recipient exposed themselves to the danger of deposition.[65]

§ 4. *The Church in the East*

At a Council held at Dovin (554), the question of simony in the hearing of confessions was brought up for the first time.[66] Besides condemning this abuse, the fathers launched an attack upon the custom of imparting blessings to which stipends were attached.[67] As neither the Fifth nor the Sixth Ecumenical Council had passed canons relative to discipline, the emperor Justinian II succeeded in having a Council convoked at Constantinople. This was called the *Concilium Quinisextum* or *Trullanum II*. One hundred and two canons pertaining to the organization and good order of the Church were passed, but couched in a language denoting great aversion and bitterness of feeling toward the Latin people. An abuse had crept into the Greek Church of charging a fee for the distribution of Holy Communion, and the fathers of the Council in rather indignant terms forbade the continuation of such a practice.[68]

From the canons of the Second Nicene Council it would seem that human ingenuity went to the extreme in seeking self aggrandizement by traffic in holy things. Bishops had gone so

---

[63] C. 2—Mansi, IX, 839.

[64] *Epist.* liii (alias lxxvi)—*MPG* 32, 386-389.

[65] C. 8—Mansi, *loc. cit.*

[66] Weber, *History of Simony*, p. 143.

[67] C. 19, 26—Mai, *Script. Vet. Nova Collectio*, X, 275.

[68] C. 22, 23—Mansi, XI, 954. Canon 23 is found in the *Corpus Juris Canonici*, c. 100, C. I, q. 1, but is attributed to the sixth synod or the Third Council of Constantinople.

far as to penalize clerics, to halt the sacred ministry, and even to close the churches because certain exactions were not forthcoming. In the light of such conditions, it is hardly necessary to say that sacred orders had their price. The desire of pious souls to embrace the monastic life also furnished a source of revenue to unscrupulous persons. But the measures adopted by the Nicene Council were direct and drastic. Bishops who sought to augment their fortunes by unscrupulous taxation were condemned. Those who had purchased their positions and dignities were to be demoted to the lowest place, and if they did not make amends, they were to be fined.[69] Intermediaries, if clerics, were to be deposed, and if laics, anathematized. Nothing was to be exacted for admission to the monastic life, and for persistent violation of this rule, a bishop, a prefect of a monastery, or a priest was to be deposed according to the decrees of the Council of Chalcedon. An abbess who disregarded this canon, was to be reduced to the rank of a subordinate and transferred to another monastery. The same punishment was to be meted out to the prefect of a monastery who was not a priest. In spite of the vigor of these laws, it would seem that the Council did not forbid the acceptance of money from the parents of the novice, nor from the person himself.[70] On the contrary, it not only allowed such gifts, but decreed that such gifts were to remain the property of the monastery, even though the religious would depart, unless there be complaint against the superior.

The activity against simony was not confined wholly to the Oriental Church in communion with Rome. Traces of similar opposition can be found even among the sects. Thus, when one Abraham was simoniacally consecrated Nestorian bishop of *Beith Lāphat*, in the south of Persia, both he and his three consecrators were excommunicated by two succeeding patriarchs.[71] The

[69] Cc. 4, 5—Mansi, XII, 951.

[70] Thomassinus, *Vetus et Nova Disciplina,* VII, c. 52, n. 10.

[71] Wigran, *An Introduction to the History of the Assyrian Church,* p. 193. The influence of outside forces is pointed out by Fowler (*Christian Egypt,* pp. 76, 98). Concerning the introduction of simony into Egypt he says that the Coptic patriarch, Michael III (881-884), was forced to exact large sums of money from bishops-elect to meet the demands of the Mussulman government and that the system continued for several hundred years.

Council of Seleucia-Ctesiphon, in the year 576, with equal vehemence condemned under pain of deposition, those who secured benefices through secular influences; and laymen who acted as mediators were excommunicated.[72] In the legislation of the various countries there will be noticed a certain uniformity. Definite enactments had been made concerning practically all the sacraments, benefices, such as they were, religious profession and many of the sacramentals. Whether the consequent laws were the effect of abuses or merely measures of precaution must be left to the historian. It will be sufficient for the present study to note the progress of the evolution, the gradual clarification of the meaning of the spiritual object which, by the will of God or of His Church, is beyond the pale of commercialism.

§ 5. *Simony in Roman Law*

The Roman Emperors looked with favor upon the Church's efforts to stamp out venality in the acquisition of bishoprics, and lent the aid of their own sanctions against the avaricious. Up to this point, simony had been considered an ecclesiastical crime, punishable by the penalties enacted by Pontiffs and Councils. At the time of Leo I (457-474) the abuse assumed an additional civil character. In an edict addressed to the Prefect Armasius, issued in the year 469, during the consulships of Zeno and Marcianus, the Emperor Leo declared that the procuring of the episcopate through pecuniary influence was to be considered a public crime against the State, equivalent to lese-majesty or treason, carrying with it the deprivation of episcopal dignity and perpetual infamy.[73] In the same category was included the acceptance of remuneration for ordination or election. In the West, a similar attitude was adopted by Glycerius, in an edict addressed to Himelco (473), pretorian prefect of Italy.[74] Bishops had appropriated to themselves the revenues of certain churches, and with them had rewarded their adherents, and even sold goods destined for the poor. It is worthy

---

[72] Chabot, *Syndicon Orientale*, 355-357, 386.

[73] Code I, iii, 30 (31), 5-6.

[74] *Corpus Legum ab Imperatoribus Romanis Ante Justinianum Latarum* (ed. Haenel, Lipsiae, 1857), p. 260.

of note that the Emperor attributed the misfortunes with which Rome had been visited, to the cupidity and avarice of these prelates. Glycerius took steps to eradicate the evil. A bishop who secured his office through worldly influence was to be deprived of his See after a year. During this year, an imperial officer was to carry on the administration of the ecclesiastical affairs. The consecrator of a simoniacal bishop was to be deprived of his bishopric; the citizens of the town who had been influenced by pecuniary motives rather than by the talents of the candidate were to be banished from the land and were to pay a fine equivalent to the sum received for the illicit election. Not only clerics, but all Christians were to be admitted as witnesses, and a suitable reward was to be paid for testimony which secured the conviction of the offenders.

Justinian was vigorous in his attacks upon simony. In the year 528, he issued an edict to the Prefect Atarbius, in which he dwelt at length upon the qualifications necessary for the episcopate and priesthood.[75] He renewed the provisions of the Council of Chalcedon by forbidding venality even in the acquisition of offices which did not require ordination. The loss of the dignity or office thus acquired was the penalty for infractions of this statute.

In his "Novels," Justinian continues his exposition of the qualities requisite for sacred offices. He cited an abuse which had been brought up at the Council of Nicea.[76] Clerics, not satisfied with the churches or provinces for which they had been ordained, cast envious eyes upon more lucrative appointments. They went so far as to make overtures in a pecuniary way for the larger and more prosperous stations. Justinian forbade the transfer of clerics without the express approval of the patriarch or the emperor, unless such a change was made necessary by a vacancy.[77] Even though a candidate possessed the qualifications necessary for the office, the mere fact that he had resorted to bribery to secure it, rendered him ineligible, and both he and his consecrator were deprived of their dignity. The one who had

---

[75] Code, I, iii, 41 (42), 1-16.

[76] Cc. 15, 16—Mansi, 674-675.

[77] Novel III, c. ii, pr.; CXXIII, c. ix.

received the money was bound to restore it to the Church which had suffered the indignity. Laymen were to pay double the amount they had received for their support; government officials, besides losing their positions were exiled forever. In order to fill candidates with a greater horror for dishonesty and cupidity, the Emperor ordered that they be placed before the people on the day of their ordination or election, and that the enactments and sanctions of the law be read to them in the presence of the faithful. Then, if any one has any complaint against them, he should come forward. In which case, the ordination or election is to be deferred until an investigation may be made. Should the parties proceed to the ordination without the necessary inquiries, both are to be deposed. Anyone making a false accusation is to be excommunicated forever.[78]

The clergy were forbidden to exact an admission tax from the newly appointed priests. Violations were punished by deposition of the offender and the installation of the applicant in his place. This regulation did not apply to the city of Constantinople, although the advocates of that city were held responsible for the enforcement of the law, and upon conviction of negligence were to be fined ten pounds.[79] Exception was made however, for the cathedraticum or gifts which bishops were wont to give upon the occasion of their consecration and installation. Justinian regulated by statute the amount of such gifts, which were to be in proportion to the revenues of the church. Bishops whose revenues were less than two gold pounds were forbidden to make such gifts.[80]

As a final touch toward the purification of episcopal elections, Justinian demanded that the electors take an oath that their choice was not prompted by gifts, promises, friendship, favor or any other motive. The bishop-elect was to swear that he neither gave nor promised anything either personally nor through another, and that he would not give anything to his consecrator, the electors or any other person. Violations of

---

[78] Novel VI, c. ii, 9-10.

[79] Novel LVI, c. i; CXIII, pr.

[80] Novel CXXIII, c. iii.

this statute were to be punished with deposition both for the consecrator and the elected.[81]

Article IV.—From the Twelfth to the Seventeenth Century

With the knowledge of the conditions in various localities, our study can now direct its attention to the laws which centered about particular institutions. Legislation had become sufficiently crystallized, to allow the grouping of laws about individual objects of abuse.

§ 1. *Benefices*

Before the fifth century, there is no trace of ecclesiastical benefices in history. Every cleric received his sustenance at the hands of his superior. Distribution of ecclesiastical goods for the use of the Church and its ministers was not regulated by law, but was entrusted to the bishops. At such a time, these methods were possible, owing to the community of life existing between the bishop and his clergy. As the possessions of the Church increased, dissentions arose concerning their distribution. An attempt was made to appease the parties by a system of dividing the fruits into four parts, one of which became the property of the bishop, another that of the cleric, a third was devoted to the expenses of religion and a fourth was given to the poor.[82] This remained the rule until such time as the increase of the number of clerics or of the immovable goods of the Church made it necessary to adopt other methods.[83]

In the ninth century, the practice of attaching permanently a certain amount of temporal goods to the pastoral office was begun. The revenues were to furnish the incumbent with a means of livelihood. By the eleventh century, community of life among the clergy began to disappear, and this brought about a division of ecclesiastical goods so that a certain amount was

---

[81] Novel CXXXVII, c. ii.

[82] C. 23, 26, 27, 28, 30, C. XII, q. 2.

[83] C. 5, 7, 8, C. X, q. 1; cf. Wernz, *Jus Decretalium*, II, n. 245; Cocchi, *Commentarium*, lib. III, pars V, n. 79.

attached to each office, thus giving a great impetus to the development of the system of benefices.[84]

The word *benefice* had a varied meaning, including all offices to which was attached the *munus ordinarium*. The notions seem to have been borrowed from the custom of military Rome, of giving booty to soldiers who had distinguished themselves in battle. Soldiers who received such gifts from their commanders were called *beneficiaries*, while the gifts themselves were known as *benefices*.[85] In the Church, the word benefice included not only bishoprics, but also deaneries, canonries, parishes, rectorships, generalships, abbacies, provincialships, priories[86] and even the allowances which were given to clerics for the pursuance of their studies.[87]

As early as the ninth century, the Church had begun her war upon the illicit acquisition of benefices. The Councils of Arles and Vienne forbade both clerics and laymen to charge anything for securing a benefice.[88] During the period under consideration the measures were drastic. At the beginning of the twelfth century deposition was the penalty for securing a benefice through purchase.[89] Forfeiture of dignity and office[90] and anathema were soon to follow.[91] In this, as in other simoniacal practices, a feeble attempt to evade the law was made by appealing to custom. The second Council of the Lateran[92] (1139) expressly stated that contrary customs were to be abolished, adding that the penalty of infamy in law was to

---

[84] Schmalzgrueber, *Jus Ecclesiasticum Universum*, lib. III, tit. V, n. 2; Garcia, *De Beneficiis Ecclesiasticis*, I, c. I, n. 10; Ayrinhac, *Constitution of the Church*, pp. 296, 311.

[85] Santi, *Praelectiones Juris Canonici*, lib. III, tit. V, n. 2; Golden *Parochial Benefices*, p. 3.

[86] Ballerini-Palmieri, *Opus Theologicum Morale*, II, tr. VI, n. 322.

[87] Zallinger, *Institutiones*, lib. V, tit. III, n. 82.

[88] VI Arles (813), c. 5; Vienne (888), c. 4—Thomassinus, *Vetus et Nova Disciplina*, VII, c. 58, nn. 3, 7.

[89] Council of Poitiers (1100), c. 2—Mansi, XX, 1123.

[90] Council of London IV (1127), c. 1—Mansi, XXI, 355.

[91] Council of Rheims (1119), c. 1—Mansi, XXI, 235.

[92] C. 2—Mansi, XXI, 526.

be imposed, whether the money was received before or after the conferring of the benefice.

A deplorable condition was cited by Innocent III at the third Lateran Council. When the rectorship of a church was vacant, some bishops placed the churches under interdict, and would not permit another rector to be appointed until a certain sum of money had been paid.[93] The Pontiff expressly forbade such a practice, and stated that prelates who had charged these prices would be obliged to restore double the amount,[94] which was to be devoted to the use of the church which had been thus outraged.

When a man was presented to a benefice and found worthy, the bishop could not delay his installation longer than two months, in the hope of securing the fruits of the benefice during the vacancy. Otherwise, he would be obliged to restore to the candidate the fruits which had accrued during this time. He could, however, demand that the candidate depose on oath that his presentation was free of simony.[95] At this point might be mentioned the very definite legislation of the Spanish Church upon simony in benefices. Laymen guilty of this crime were excommunicated. A cleric who possessed no benefice was considered irregular for two years, while one who was in possession of a benefice was suspended until he had restored double the amount, half of which was to go to the Church, and the other half was to be sent to the cathedral. Bishops, patrons or even

---

[93] "Quod facere non poterant, tum quia pro causa civili non debat Ecclesia interdicto subjici: tum ne impediatur sacramentorum administratio."—Gonzalez, *Commentarium Perpetuum,* lib. V, tit. III, n. 40; cf. also tit. XXXVII, c. 3, n. 1.

[94] C. 41, X, *de simonia,* V, 3. This, at first sight, might seem to be a contradiction of those texts where restitution of the amount received was imposed, without any additional sum in penalty. Gonzalez (*Commentarium Perpetuum,* lib. V, tit. III, c. 40, n. 4) attempts to explain the matter by saying that in cases where there was a contract between the giver and the receiver, simply the amount paid was to be restored; but the present text is occupied not with a voluntary stipulation on the part of the giver, but rather with an extortion by the superior. Hence the penalty for the transgression.

[95] Council of Oxford (1222), cc. 4, 17—Mansi, XXII, 1151, 1158.

notaries who charged for their services would incur suspension for six months.[96]

Paul II, in his constitution "*Cum detestabile,*"[97] issued 2 Nov. 1464, decreed excommunication *latae sententiae* against those guilty of simony in benefices together with their mediators. Some are inclined to think that the words of Paul refer only to those who are direct intermediaries, and exclude all who merely counselled the action. However, the more probable opinion seems to be that all who in any way cooperated in simoniacal traffic in benefices are affected by this censure.[98] Not only was the title to the benefice null and void, whether the fault had been committed by the beneficiary or another, but the same condition obtained even if the beneficiary had been ignorant of the illicit transaction. Upon him devolved the obligation of resigning the benefice and restoring the fruits thereof.[99] One who had simoniacally come into possession of a benefice was irregular and the bishop could not absolve him from this irregularity unless he had been inculpably ignorant of the simony. In the latter case the bishop could release him, if the simony had been committed in a simple benefice, i.e. one which did not carry with it the administration of the sacraments or the care of souls, but it was essential that he resign all claim to the benefice.[100] Reiffenstuel[101] advances the opinion that if the crime had not received sentence in the external forum the bishop could dispense. In the canon cited, the words *illa vice* were used in restricting the power of the bishop. This led Suarez[102] to conclude that if the benefice were once given to another person and afterwards became vacant, the bishop could

[96] Council of Valencia in the diocese of Sabina, (1322), c. 19—Mansi, XXV, 714.

[97] C. 2, *de simonia,* V, 1, in Extravag. com. The *Bullarium Romanum* (tom. V, pp. 16-17) attributes this to Eugene IV, 18 May, 1434.

[98] *Nouvelle Revue Théologique,* IX (1887), 386.

[99] This provision has been retained in the present law. Cf. canon 729, and Chapter III of this dissertation.

[100] C. 59, X *de electione,* I, 6; cf. Suarez, *Opera Omnia,* tom. XIII, lib. IV, c. 61, n. 10.

[101] *Jus Canonicum Universum,* lib. V, tit. III, n. 337.

[102] *Opera Omnia,* tom. XIII, lib. IV, c. 61, n. 10.

dispense the one who had been guilty of simony, and he would be able to receive the benefice.

The constitution of Pius V, "*Cum primum,*" [103] 1 April 1566, would seem to have settled once and for all the question of the power of the bishop in dispensing from such irregularities. The Pontiff expressly declared that those who were guilty of simony in benefices were to be considered perpetually ineligible, not only for that one, but for any benefice whatsoever. Nevertheless, there seems to have arisen a custom contrary to this law, which secured legitimate prescription, whereby no dispensation was required as long as the crime had not been sentenced.[104]

The Council of Trent[105] expressly forbade examiners for benefices to accept anything on the occasion of an examination. The penalty for violation of this rule was the sanctions which the law placed upon simony, and the violators were not to be absolved unless they had resigned whatever benefices they had, and were to become ineligible for others. Paul IV, in his *motu proprio,* "*Inter caeteras,*"[106] 27 Nov. 1557, cited a custom whereby one would secure a benefice by pretending he was someone else, intending to transfer it to that person in exchange for a portion of the revenues. The Pontiff in vigorous terms condemned those persons, no matter of what dignity, whether cleric or lay, who lent themselves to such a practice, and established the penalty of excommunication to be incurred *ipso facto,* and reserved to the Holy See in such a manner that outside of the actual danger of death it could be absolved by no one except the Pope himself.

About the time of Pius IV another and more insidious form of simony was in existence. When the subject for whom a person of influence wished to secure a benefice was juridically ineligible, ambitious persons soon found a means of safeguarding themselves and circumventing the law. They bestowed the benefice upon someone else, with the understanding that he was

---

[103] *Fontes,* n. 111.

[104] Suarez, *loc. cit.,* c. 58, n. 11.

[105] Sess. XXIV, *de ref.,* c. 18.

[106] *Fontes,* n. 92.

to resign in favor of the one who secured it or in favor of a third party. When the impediment was removed, the party who had been hitherto ineligible received the benefice through the resignation of the holder. This was called confidential simony.[107] Pius IV cited several Cardinals as having been guilty of this crime. To abolish the practice, the Pope declared that in the future Cardinals and other prelates found guilty of this sort of simony, were to be interdicted from entrance to the Church, while persons of lesser dignity were to incur *ipso facto* major excommunication reserved to the Sovereign Pontiff, from which no one could absolve except *in articulo mortis*. The collation of such benefices was declared null and void, their disposition was reserved to the Holy See and their pensions or revenues were to be applied to the Apostolic Camera.[108]

In renewing the provisions of the constitution of Pius IV Pope Pius V enumerated some of the reasons for the prevalence of confidential simony.[109] Many could not legally hold benefices; others did not want to receive sacred orders nor to undertake the obligation of residence nor to assume the clerical habit. Some did not wish to relinquish their military status; others were ineligible from some crime. The Pope renewed the provisions of Pius IV and in a secret consistory on 14 Nov. 1569, extended all the penalties to Cardinals.[110] The Constitutions of Pius IV and Pius V remained the law until Sixtus V modified the provisions regarding the disposition of simoniacal benefices. The latter Pontiff permitted the collation of such benefices to the Ordinaries as long as the Bishops had not participated in nor consented to the crime.[111]

---

107 Exchange of benefices must be placed in the category with common simony, even though it might contain the various reservations with which confidential simony is identified. The documents which concerned themselves with the suppression of confidential simony did not mention the exchange of benefices and hence this abuse cannot be considered as a form of confidential simony. Cf. Reiffenstuel, *Jus Canonicum Universum*, lib. V, tit. III, n. 39.

108 Const. "*Romanum Pontificem*," 17 oct. 1564, §§ 1-4—*Fontes*, n. 106.

109 Const. "*Intolerabilis*," 1 jun. 1569—*Fontes*, n. 130.

110 Const. "*Hodie*," 14 nov. 1569—Fontes, n. 131.

111 Const. "*Pastoralis officii*," 13 aug. 1587—*Bullarium Romanum*, VIII, 895.

The thirty-sixth rule of the Apostolic Chancery of Calistus III[112] provided that anyone possessing a benefice for a period of three years, even though his title were null and void, would be considered to have secured legitimate prescription, unless simony had been committed in its acquisition. Authors disputed whether this rule would bind in the case of triennial possession in good faith, where the simony had been committed by a third person, without the knowledge of the beneficiary. Some[113] defended such a possession upon the principle that the rule should be interpreted broadly in so far as it is favorable, and strictly in so far as it is unfavorable. Leinz[114] contended that the interpretation which excuses the possessor in good faith from the effects of the law is at least contrary to the spirit of canon law. The Church has ever been inimical to the simoniacal acquisition of benefices, making exception only for those upon whom fraud had been practiced or who had protested against simony from the beginning. In other cases, he says, the guiding principle must be: "quod initio vitiosum est, non potest tractu temporis convalescere."[115] His opinion would seem to be the more probable in view of the fact that the Church has always insisted upon the resignation of those whose acquisition of a benefice had been tainted with simony, even when the crime had been committed by a third party.

§ 2. *Ordinations*

Deposition had been a frequent penalty for those who sought orders by purchase, as well as for those who offered them for gain. Gregory IX[116] attached to simony in orders suspension for three years and inability to receive higher orders, both of which penalties were reserved to the Holy See. This sanction affected not only the candidate, but also the one who presented

---

[112] Rigantius, *Commentarium in Regulas,* III, n. 132, p. 190.

[113] Reiffenstuel, *Jus Canonicum Universum,* lib. V, tit. III, n. 278; Suarez, *Opera Omnia,* tom. XIII, lib. IV, c. 57, n. 9; Santi, *Praelectiones Juris Canonici,* lib. V, tit. III, n. 30.

[114] *Die Simonie,* p. 123.

[115] Digest, XXIX, 50, 17.

[116] C. 45, X, *de simonia,* V, 3.

him, as well as the prelate who conferred the orders. The Council of Trent[117] forbade even the acceptance of voluntary oblations on the occasion of ordinations and the conferring of first tonsure. The Fathers ratified all the previous enactments against simony in ordinations. Immediately following the Council, the question arose whether it had been its intention to extend the penalties for simony in orders to the simoniacal conferring of tonsure. Previous legislation had mentioned orders, and strictly speaking tonsure is not included under that term. Some[118] concluded that while the Council wished to forbid the acceptance of offerings for first tonsure as well as for orders, the penalties were to be incurred only by those who simoniacally conferred orders, properly so called. The doubt was settled, however, by Sixtus V[119] who expressly declared that the penalties applied also to those who conferred first tonsure. The Pontiff extended the ten-year suspension imposed by Pius V[120] to perpetuity, and absolution was removed from the competence of Bishops even when the crime was occult. Outside of the *articulus mortis*, not even the Sacred Penitentiary could absolve. This law of Sixtus V remained practically unchanged until the time of Pius IX and the issuance of the constitution *"Apostolicae Sedis."*

§ 3. *Entrance to Religion*

During the persecutions, especially that of Decius in the third century, the early Christians fled for safety into the desert places. Singly or in groups they remained there, spending their time in labor and communion with God. When the storm had passed, they had grown to love the solitude and silence, where they could pray in peace, far from the turmoil of the world. They remained, and their life soon attracted others, until an institution was formed which was to occupy a prominent place in the world. Such were the lowly beginnings of monasticism.

117 Sess. XXI, *de ref.*, c. 1.

118 Cf. St. Alphonsus, *Theologia Moralis*, lib. III, n. 110.

119 Const. *"Sanctum et salutare,"* 5 jan. 1589, § 6—*Fontes*, n. 166.

120 Const. *"Cum primum,"* 1 apr. 1566, § 8—*Fontes*, n. 111.

But as the little bands of monks became augmented with the passage of time, their labors, bearing the fruit of toil mingled with a consciousness of God's presence, brought them into possession of the goods of this world. Their opulence was a matter of time and with riches came evil. They attracted the attention of those envious souls who are ever watchful of an opportunity of securing an easy livelihood, and who would go to any extreme to attain their desires. On the other hand, possibly where the monastery or convent was not so well endowed, some unscrupulous regulars saw in the holy desires of man to embrace the religious state, a chance for self emolument. Simony in admission to the religious state became a problem.[121]

The profession itself was certainly a holy and spiritual thing. The religious state was equally spiritual. Hence the bartering of these was sufficient to constitute simony.[122] The usual plea in defense of such abuses was the poverty of the monastery. From the earliest times, the Popes and Councils sought to remove the effect by suppressing the cause. They aimed directly at the root of the trouble, by forbidding monasteries to accept any more candidates than might be supported from the ordinary revenues of the institution. By limiting the number of religious to the size of the resources they left no excuse for charging an admission fee.[123] The Fourth Council of the Lateran[124] (1215) scored the venality of those nuns who, under the pretext of poverty would not admit candidates to their convent unless they paid a certain fee.[125] In order to curb this evil, the Council

[121] For a more intensive study of the activities of the early monks, cf. Maitland, *The Dark Ages*, p. 2; Newman, *Historical Sketches*, II, 365; Shahan, "The Middle Ages," *American Catholic Quarterly*, XI (1886), 597; *The Catholic World*, CXVII (1923), 477, LXXXVIII (1908), 90; *Revue Benedictine*, VIII (1891), 1-49.

[122] Zallinger, *Institutiones*, lib. V, tit. III, n. 91.

[123] Thomassinus, *Vetus et Nova Disciplina*, VII, c. 50.

[124] C. 64—Mansi XXII, 1051.

[125] Suarez (*Opera Omnia*, tom. XIII, lib. IV, c. 17) cites Navarrus as explaining this text to apply to nuns who received more than what was required for the entrant's support. Gibalinus (*De Simonia*, q. 18, c. 9), however, takes the view that the Council had in mind those who exacted money not as a means of support but as an actual entrance fee.

decreed that in the future anyone guilty of this abuse must be transferred to another monastery of stricter discipline, there to do perpetual penance without hope of being restored to his original place. Those whose crime antedated the Council, should be transferred to another monastery of the same order. If this were not possible without grave inconvenience, on account of the small number of monks or nuns, the delinquents might be permitted to remain on condition that they be removed from whatever places of honor they might occupy and be demoted to more lowly stations.

This price of admission must not be confused with the dowry which nuns were allowed to demand in addition to the expenses of the novitiate, for the latter was not an entrance fee, but rather a means of support for the religious.[126] Gratuitous admission had been followed by numerous abuses, for parents often forced their daughters to enter religion, that they might be spared the expense of their support. Then, too, nuns who led a contemplative life were without other means of subsistence.[127]

With reference to the monasteries of men, while the general rule seems to have been that they were forbidden to exact anything beyond the expenses of the novitiate,[128] there seems to have been at least a probable opinion that in the case of a poor monastery something might be exacted, not as a price of admission to the religious state, but as a means of support for the entrant.[129]

The penalties which were established for violations of the law during this period were severe. Excommunication reserved to the Sovereign Pontiff was incurred by those who demanded

---

[126] S. C. Ep. et Reg., *Spoletana,* 17 jul. 1574—*Fontes,* n. 1313; *Asculana,* 1 mart. 1580—*Fontes,* n. 1366; S.C.C., *Belgii,* 18 sept. 1683—*Fontes,* n. 2875.

[127] Schäfer, *Compendium de Religiosis,* n. 228.

[128] Conc. Trident., sess. XXV, *de regularibus,* c. 16; *Collectanea in usum Sec. S. C. Ep. et Reg.,* p. 396, 439; S. C. Ep. et Reg., *Carmelitarum,* 11 dec. 1789—*Fontes,* n. 1884.

[129] St. Thomas, *Summa Theologica,* 2, 2, q. 100, art. 3, ad. 4; Raymond of Pennafort, *Summa,* lib. I, tit. I, n. 14; Lessius, *De Justitia et Jure,* lib. III, c. 35, n. 71; St. Alphonsus, *Theologia Moralis,* lib. III, n. 91.

payment and those who gave it,[130] and if the convent or chapter consented to the transaction, the entire body incurred *ipso facto* suspension. The parties concerned were to be removed to a stricter monastery and to undergo perpetual penance. This latter punishment was abrogated by the silence of the constitution "*Solet annuere*"[131] of Innocent IV, 19 Aug. 1253.

§ 4. *Simony in Other Things*

Three principal abuses occupied a prominent place in the contest of the Church against simony, viz. traffic in benefices, in ordinations and in the religious profession. From time to time she was forced to raise her voice against other abuses. The exaction of money for the dedication of churches, chrism and the holy oils, the blessing of marriages and burial services and the sacraments was vigorously opposed.[132] Alexander III cited an abuse which was quite startling. Upon the payment of a sum of money certain priests were appointed deans. They in turn would exercise jurisdiction in the name of the bishop, charging fees for their services. The Pope declared that if this practice should continue, the bishop would be deprived of his power of appointing deans.[133] At the Fourth Lateran Council (1215) it was shown to what extremes the cupidity of some priests had gone.[134] They were accustomed to demand certain fees for burials, marriages, etc., and if they were not satisfied with the amount received, they immediately found some fictitious impediment as a pretext upon which to refuse their services. While commending the proper observance of pious customs, the Pope forbade priests to resort to such conduct to secure the stole fees.[135]

---

[130] C. 1, *de simonia,* V, 1, in Extravag. com.

[131] *Bullarium Romanum,* XXXII, 570. From the fact that the delinquents were not allowed to return to the world, it would seem that the profession was valid. Cf. Zallinger, *Institutiones,* lib. V, tit. III, n. 103; St. Thomas, *Summa Theologica,* 2, 2, q. 100, art. 6, ad 5; Boniface VIII (c. 1, *de statu regularium,* III, 16, in VI°) apparently declared the simoniacal profession invalid.

[132] C. 10, 16, 29, 42, X, *de simonia,* V, 3.

[133] C. 1, X, *ne praelati vices suas,* V, 4.

[134] C. 63-64—c. 42, X, *de simonia,* V, 3.

[135] In a letter to the Archbishop of Canterbury, Innocent III refers to a

Before passing to what might be termed more recent legislation, a word must be said concerning a source of simony which played an important part in the Lutheran revolt. It is not the purpose of this study to consider in detail the nature of indulgences, nor to vindicate to the Church the power of granting them. Such a digression would carry the work too far afield. It will be sufficient to note that no indulgence can under any circumstances, be gained by a person who is not in the state of grace. Even the simplest of the Church's pardons requires as its indispensable preliminary, that the sinner be reconciled with God. Hence, with but a moment's reflection it will be seen that an indulgence is not a remission of sin, nor a license to commit sin, as has been frequently alleged. The point which is of more immediate interest is the abuses which crept into the granting of indulgences, and the measures adopted by the Church in eradicating them.

Almsgiving may be considered as one of the good works often required to gain an indulgence. Even the least among the people understood that the giving of an alms for charitable purpose was just as much a good work as the recital of prayers or the going on a pilgrimage to some shrine.[136] The Popes and Bishops entrusted the publication of the indulgences to itinerant preachers, known as *praedicatores quaestuosi* or *quaestores*, and upon these men devolved the collection of alms. The Fourth Lateran Council recommends discretion to the *quaestores*, and prescribes a form which they should use in offering the spiritual favors and inviting the generosity of the faithful.[137] The general complaint seems to have been that the quaestors did not remain within the bounds of truth in their preaching.[138] The

---

novel means of evading the law, which was practiced in England. The taking of money for the holy oils had been forbidden repeatedly. Hence to circumvent the prohibition, a custom had been introduced of receiving the customary Holy Thursday offerings about the middle of Lent. The name was accordingly changed from *chrismal offerings* to *paschal offerings.* Cf. c. 36, X, *de simonia,* V, 3.

[136] Thurston, "The Medieval Pardoner," *The Month,* CXLII (1923), 522-532; Newman, *Present Position of Catholics in England,* p. 113.

[137] Mansi, XXII, 1052.

[138] C. 1-3, *de poenitentiis et remissionibus,* V, 10, in VI°.

Council of Mainz[139] (1261) took up the question of the abuses of the *quaestores.* On account of the scandal they had caused, the Fathers forbade the clergy to admit them to the churches, under pain of suspension. Privilege was granted to bishops to make use of the services of these preachers on occasion, when the cause was legitimate, but their coming was to be without pomp and ceremony, and the clergy were ordered to explain to the people the reasons for their admission. Under no circumstances were such preachers to be welcomed without letters from the bishop, and these credentials must be inspected and proved to be genuine. Suspension *ipso facto* was the penalty for disregarding these precautions. Should the preachers become insistent, the people were authorized to appeal to the secular power, if other means for their repulsion could not be found.[140]

The Council of Trent,[141] seeing that the remedies prescribed by the Councils of the Lateran, Lyons and Vienne, against the abuses of the quaestors had been fruitless, and that they per-

---

[139] Mansi, XXIII, 1102.

[140] The Dominican, John Tetzel, is a figure around which much discussion centers, since he was the local deputy commissary and preacher of Leo the Tenth's great indulgence to provide money for the building of St. Peter's. He gave himself with a certain amount of arrogance to his work and aroused considerable opposition. Paulus (*Geschichte des Ablasses im Mittelalter,* III, 425, 495) denies the foundation of the accusations that Tetzel claimed his indulgences were a remission of sin, that he sold forgiveness of sin for money, without even mentioning confession and contrition, that he absolved from sins which might be committed in the future. That Tetzel was orthodox in his teaching can be seen from his own words: "Indulgences do not pardon sins, but only remit the temporal punishment due to sin, when the sins have been sorrowfully confessed. . . Consequently whosoever gives alms to procure an indulgence gives primarily for God's sake, seeing that no one can obtain an indulgence, who has not attained to true repentance and the love of God."—Grisar, *Luther,* I, 329. It was with regard to his notions of indulgences for the dead that he seems to have strayed from orthodox teachings. "As regard Indulgences for the dead, there is no doubt that Tetzel did, according to what he considered his authoritative instructions, proclaim as Christian doctrine that nothing but an offering of money was required to gain the Indulgence for the dead, without there being any question of contrition or confession. . . The Papal Bull of Indulgence gave no sanction whatever to this proposition."—Pastor, *History of the Popes,* VII, 349.

[141] Sess. XXI, *de ref.,* c. 9.

severed in their nefarious practices, ordained that the name of the quaestors and their methods be utterly abolished in all parts of Christendom. The Indulgences were to be published by local Ordinaries, to whom also was granted the power to collect alms, "without receiving any remuneration, so that all men may know that these heavenly treasures are administered not for gain, but for godliness." However, not even the fulminations of the Council of Trent could stop the intrepid quaestors. Hence, it became necessary for Pope Pius V to take drastic steps for their suppression. Accordingly on February 8, 1567, he issued the constitution "*Etsi Dominici*," in which he formally cancelled all concessions of indulgences involving money transactions.[142] The words of the Pope were explicit and direct. Nevertheless, within two years reports reached Rome that the provisions of the Council of Trent as well as the Pope's own constitution were disregarded in some localities, and a price was still placed upon certain indulgences and favors. The Pope then decided to settle once and for all the fate of those who trafficked in indulgences. In his constitution "*Quam plenum*,"[143] he declared that bishops and prelates or those of higher rank, including Cardinals, who were guilty of this abuse, would incur interdict from entering the church, and privation of all the fruits of their benefices, until they had made sufficient reparation. All other persons would incur excommunication reserved to the Pope. This remained the law until the promulgation of the Code.

ARTICLE V.—FROM THE SEVENTEENTH CENTURY TO THE CODE

By the seventeenth century, the laws upon simony had become crystallized. The mind of the Church had been defined clearly, and she had fulminated her most severe penalties against the guilty parties. During the period under consideration, she was

---

[142] *Fontes*, n. 118. Concerning the Spanish concessions, cf. Smith, "Bula de la Cruzada"—*The Month*, CIII (1904), 131-144, 235-242.

[143] *Fontes*, n. 132. Gasparri, in the *Fontes*, places the date of this constitution as 2 jan. 1570, though Cappello (*De Censuris*, n. 293) Pruemmer, (*Manuale Theologiae Moralis*, III, n. 514) give the same day of the preceding year.

occupied in repeating the laws which were in force, in tempering them to the needs of the times, and in calling attention to violations as occasions presented themselves.

§ 1. *The Seventeenth Century*

In an effort to palliate their misdeeds, some had put forth the claim that in conferring a benefice, the right to the temporal revenues might be separated from the office, and hence a price could be demanded for it. The fallacy of this assertion can be seen immediately if the nature of the benefice is examined. "Beneficium ecclesiasticum constitutive enasci ex unione duorum elementorum quae sunt: officium ecclesiasticum et jus ad reditus, sub essentiale conditione legitimae erectionis et quidem in perpetuum."[144] Alexander VII[145] condemned the proposition which declared that it was not against justice to demand payment for the temporalities connected with the benefice. The elements of purchase and sale were next attacked. If these could be eliminated from the contract, all comparison between the spiritual and the temporal would vanish, and the action could not be called simoniacal. Consequently, it was argued that if the money were given, not as a price, but as a motive for impelling the other person to grant a spiritual favor, there would be no simony. The same would be true if the acquisition of the temporal goods was the sole reason for granting the spiritual favor, or if the person considered the temporal of relatively greater value than the spiritual. As is apparent, the substitution of the word *motive* for *price*, does not change the substantial character of the act. If the giver did not think that his donation would be reciprocated, he would not have made the presentation at all. Furthermore, the reaction of such a person upon failure to receive what he sought, would be sufficient to convict him of simoniacal intentions, for he con-

---

[144] Cocchi, *Commentarium*, lib. III, pars V, n. 81, e. The Code (can. 727, § 1) gives the attachment of temporal goods to benefices as an example of a temporal object so annexed to the spiritual, that without it, the temporal could not exist.

[145] Denziger, *Enchiridion*, n. 993.

siders himself cheated.[146] Innocent XI[147] condemned these theses, adding that even in the case where the exchange were effected out of gratitude, there would be simony. It is the common opinion, however, that the Pontiff meant such gratitude which was strengthened by mutual agreement. If the parties would make a contract concerning what was already due from the natural obligation of gratitude, a double obligation would be imposed, the one arising from the natural law, the other from the contract. If, on the other hand, the giving of the spiritual object were prompted by pure gratitude for a favor received, there would be no simony. It is the adding of the new obligation to the one already existing, that was condemned by the Pope.[148]

In an attempt to secure uniformity, the Sacred Congregation of the Council under the inspiration of Innocent XI, issued the *Taxa Innocentiana*,[149] which stated when it was permitted to charge or accept fees for ecclesiastical services, together with the amount allowed by law. As will be seen below, some immediately began to excuse themselves on the ground that the *Taxa* applied only to Italy, and those outside of that country were free to follow their own opinions.[150]

§ 2. *The Eighteenth Century*

The Bishop of Vasion, in a synod held in the year 1729, drew up a schedule of taxes for his diocese. In this schedule was the notice that at the time of baptism, the godfather or godmother should supply at least one candle and a clean white cloth for the ceremonies. In lieu of these they might pay a stipulated sum of money. Doubts arose concerning the legality of such

---

[146] St. Alphonsus, *Theologia Moralis*, lib. III, n. 54; Schmalzgrueber, *Jus Ecclesiasticum Universum*, lib. V, tit. III, n. 73.

[147] Denziger, *Enchiridion*, nn. 1062, 1063.

[148] The sanction of Innocent XI was confirmed by Benedict XIV, in the bull "*Sollicita et provida*," 9 jul. 1753. Cf. *Bullarium Benedictinum*, X, 273.

[149] *Bullarium Romanum*, VIII, 58-61.

[150] Cf. Clement XIV, encycl. "*Decet quam maxime*," 21 sept. 1769—*Fontes*, n. 467.

a tax, and the question was proposed to the Sacred Congregation of the Council,[151] whether such a statute might remain in force. The Congregation replied with a very emphatic, *"Negative et amplius."*

An important change in the existing legislation regarding simony in ordinations and benefices took place about the middle of the eighteenth century. In the constitution *"Sanctum et salutare,"*[152] Sixtus V had removed from the Sacred Pentitentiary, as well as from the Bishops, the power to absolve from certain crimes even when occult. Among these was simony in the conferring of orders and benefices, and outside the actual danger of death, none but the Pope or his delegate could absolve. In the bull *"Pastor bonus,"*[153] Benedict XIV granted to the Major Penitentiary most ample power. Authority was conferred to absolve from all censures, in whatsoever manner reserved, whether to the Roman Pontiff, to Ordinaries or to the Superiors of Religious Orders. For regulars, this absolution was valid for the external as well as the internal forum. The same privilege was extended to seculars, both cleric and lay, when the censure was inflicted *a jure*, as would be the case of the censures of Sixtus V. It will be remembered that Sixtus V had decreed that one guilty of simony in receiving orders was to lose all hope of securing higher orders. Although the word *suspension* was used, the penalty was rather an irregularity. Benedict XIV[154] granted to the Major Penitentiary the power of dispensing from an occult irregularity, which might arise from a simoniacal contract between the ordained and his bishop. Such a dispensation, however, was confined to the internal forum. But where the simony in benefices had been committed with full knowledge (*scienter contracta*), the Pontiff bade the Sacred Penitentiary to refrain from dispensing and convalidating the title, even for the internal forum. The dispensation could be given to one who, through ignorance of

---

[151] 6 Feb. 1734—*Thesaurus Resolut. S.C.C.*, VI, 209.

[152] 5 jan. 1589—*Fontes*, n. 166.

[153] 22 apr. 1744—*Bullarium Benedicti XIV*, II, 209; cf. Martin, *The Roman Curia*, p. 122.

[154] Const. *"Pastor bonus,"* § 19

the law or of the fact, had been guilty of simony, and had made application for dispensation as soon as the fact had been brought to his knowledge.[155] According to the existing law, the price paid for the simoniacal purchase was to be restored to the church or to the poor. Benedict XIV empowered the Sacred Penitentiary to return part of the money to the person involved, if the reasons for such an action were sufficiently grave. The remaining portion was to be given to the injured church or to the poor.[156]

Clement XIV, in his encyclical to the Bishops of Sardinia, "*Decet quam maxime,*"[157] 21 Sept. 1769, has left to the world a veritable "Treatise on Simony." The Pontiff traces the legislation from the Council of Chalcedon down to the time of Innocent XI, pointing out that one of the chief sources of abuse was the toleration of contrary customs. In speaking of the *Taxa Innocentiana,* he says that even they were insufficient to restore the tottering discipline of the Church, for upon their promulgation, excuses were brought forward that the schedule was only local in character. The Pope remarks that many seemed to forget that whatever was embodied in the *Taxa* from the Sacred Canons and the Council of Trent should have been obeyed scrupulously by every ecclesiastical curia. He repeated the decrees of the Council of Trent, forbidding even free offerings at the time of ordinations, except the gift of a candle to the Bishop. The quality and weight of this candle, however, was to be left entirely to the free choice of the giver. He cited a custom which obtained in certain places of also giving a candle to the Bishop at Confirmation. Clement remarked that there was nothing in the *Pontificale* to sanction such a practice, and hence it might lead to abuses, with the result that poor people would be kept from receiving the sacrament, because they could not supply this offering.

It was often expedient to impose money fines when the character of the crime or the state of the offender might demand it. However, that all suspicion concerning the application of the

[155] *Loc. cit.,* § 22.

[156] *Loc. cit.,* § 23.

[157] *Fontes,* n. 467.

money might be removed, it is a good practice, said Clement XIV, and in some cases might even become necessary, that the pious places which were to benefit from such fines be mentioned in the written sentence. Consideration should be made for those places which are most in need, and also the domicile of person who pays the fine.[158]

With all her invectives against the purchase and sale of spiritual things, the Church did not condemn, but rather encouraged, voluntary offerings for the support of her ministers. However, she was solicitous lest these customs degenerate into abuses, and although the receipt of alms was a vital factor in the continuation of her ministry, she never hesitated to censure one who would impede the administration of the sacraments because the fees were not paid. From time to time, the Church sprang to the defense of pious customs which her enemies would have called simoniacal practices. Thus, Pius VI did not hesitate to condemn the 54th proposition of the Synod of Pistoja,[159] which declared that the accepting of mass stipends was contrary to the mind of the Apostolic Church, and an evil custom which was shielded by later Pontiffs.

§ 3. *The Nineteenth Century*

The nineteenth century is particularly interesting to the Church in the United States because of the Plenary Councils of Baltimore, and to the world because of the important changes brought about in the general law concerning censures by the promulgation of the constitution *"Apostolicae Sedis"* of Pius IX.

On April 13, 1807, the Sacred Congregation of the Propaganda[160] issued a decree extending the general legislation, with some modifications, to the patriarchate of Chaldea. Absolution from the major excommunication and suspension, as well as dispensation from the irregularity, were to be sought from the

---

[158] *Loc. cit.*, § 39.

[159] Const. *"Auctorem fidei,"* 28 aug. 1794—*Fontes*, n. 475.

[160] *Collectanea S.C. P. F.*, n. 692.

Apostolic Delegate. From time to time provincial councils[161] in Europe made reference to simoniacal practices, but added no new penalties. Kenrick[162] cites a custom in the United States, of charging for burial places, and the collection of fees either by the sexton or the pastor on the occasion of an interment. Such practices, he says, are hard to reconcile with the existing legislation. Many tried to vindicate their actions by appealing to custom and the necessity of securing money to meet the expenses of the church and cemetery.

i. *The Plenary Councils of Baltimore*

The word *simony* seems to have been avoided purposely by the Fathers of the Councils of Baltimore, probably on account of the opprobrium which was connected with the term. But from the language in which their decisions are couched, it is quite clear at what abuses their laws were aimed. The exaction of money for the administration of the sacraments, or any negotiations whatsoever concerning them, was absolutely forbidden.[163] However, the priest was permitted according to approved custom, to accept voluntary offerings on the occasion of baptisms and marriages. Stipends for masses were allowed according to the mind of the Church, but with the express understanding that the money was to be considered not as the price or compensation for the Holy Sacrifice, but as an alms for the support of the priest.[164] The fixing of the amount of the stipend should be left to the judgment of the Ordinary, if synodal law or custom had not settled the matter, according to the decision of the Sacred Congregation of the Council.[165] The Second Plenary Council made no attempt to fix the amount of the stipend for the entire country, because of the widely divergent conditions in various localities. The matter was left to the individual ordinaries, upon this condition, that once the

[161] Provincial Council of Paris, (1849)—*Collectio Lacensis,* IV, 26; Provincial Council of Sens, (1850), *loc. cit.*, IV, 888.

[162] *Theologia Moralis,* II, tr. 12, c. 6, n. 69.

[163] *Acta et Decreta C. P. Baltimor. II,* (1866), n. 221.

[164] *Loc. cit.*, n. 369. Cf. Benedict XIV, *De Sacrificio Missae,* lib. III, c. 21, n. 11, 12.

[165] S. C. C., *Aprutina,* 15 nov. 1698—Fontes, n. 2967.

stipend had been determined, the priest should neither demand more nor accept less than the statute required.[166] It seems that the latter part of this provision should be interpreted according to various circumstances, for nothing was farther from the mind of the Church than that a priest should refuse the benefit of a mass to those who could not afford to pay the full stipend. Very probably the Fathers had in mind those priests who, in order to secure stipends, would agree to say mass for less than the stipulated amount.

The Council[167] scored another abuse which had caused much unfavorable comment outside the Church. While admitting the necessity of sometimes imposing the giving of alms as a penance, confessors were strictly forbidden to apply these pecuniary penances to their own advantage. They were not permitted to ask nor to receive anything for their services in the confessional. Even the accepting of Mass stipends or other voluntary offerings in the confessional was prohibited. Strict adherence to the canons regarding burial fees was also enjoined. Should anyone desire to reserve a burial plot in a cemetery, to which he or his heirs were to have exclusive right, the Council[168] admitted that a fee might be demanded, which was to be devoted to the maintenance of the cemetery. Should any superfluous funds remain, over and above the necessary expenses, they were to be devoted to works of religion or charity according to the wishes of the Ordinary. Under no circumstances was an ecclesiastic to appropriate these funds to his own or any other use without the permission of the Bishop. An air of commerciality is often given to the divine services by the exaction of money at the doors of the church, for admission to mass on Sundays and holydays. Quite frequently, even in our own day, the only distinguishing mark between the entrance to some churches and the admission to a theatre, is the substitution of the sexton or a stalwart parishioner for the uniformed attendant, and a considerable lack of courtesy on the part of the former. Every species of excuse might be advanced for such

[166] *Acta et Decreta C. P. Baltimor. II*, n. 369.
[167] *Loc. cit.*, n. 289.
[168] *Loc. cit.*, n. 393.

a practice, nevertheless, the words of the Councils of Baltimore[169] are quite explicit and leave no opportunity for evasion. Such customs were to be discontinued, for the Fathers declared that from their own experience they knew that the Church could be supported by less scandalous means. A few years previous to the Second Plenary Council, Pope Pius IX[170] had declared that the custom of door collections was to be abolished within two years. In spite of papal and conciliar reprobations the abuse continued, as is apparent from the following extract of a letter addressed by Archbishop Falconio, Apostolic Delegate to the United States, to the American ordinaries, on September 29th, 1911:

> I, therefore, request you to command all rectors of churches in your diocese to discontinue all these practices, if they have already been introduced, and by no means to permit them to be established, if they do not already exist. I well know that in some churches money is collected at the door, not for mere entrance, but as a payment for a seat in the church. Even this practice cannot be tolerated, since it produces an undesirable impression on all, and has proved to be, in practice, the cause of many regrettable consequences.[171]

ii. *The Constitution "Apostolicae Sedis"*

In the course of centuries, penal statutes had accumulated so quickly that their number became enormous. An attempt to simplify the legislation was made by the Council of Trent. In the three hundred years which elapsed between the Council of Trent and the pontificate of Pius IX, the number of penal laws had again multiplied. The result was confusion and scruples. "In our desire to meet these difficulties," says the Pontiff, "We ordered a thorough revision of those censures to be made and placed before us, in order that on mature consideration, We might determine those which ought to be retained and observed, and those which it would be well to alter or

---

[169] *Loc. cit.*, n. 397; *Acta et Decreta C. P. Baltimor.* III, n. 288.

[170] Letter of Card. Alexander Barnabo, Prefect of S. C. de Prop. Fid., Feb. 1862—*Collectio Lacensis*, III, 229-230.

[171] *AER*, XLV (1911), 594.

abrogate."[172] From the text of the constitution, it is manifest that the intention of the Pope was to reduce to as small a number as possible, the correctional punishments, i.e., excommunications, suspensions and interdicts, which were incurred *ipso facto*. Pius IX wished to adapt the legislation to the needs of the time, for many of the ancient laws had become impractical and useless, because they had been enacted for circumstances which no longer existed. Besides the list of censures expressly mentioned in the Constitution, it was the wish of the Pontiff to renew and ratify the censures *latae sententiae* which had been enacted by the Council of Trent, and it is this provision which gave rise to many difficulties. What censures of the Council of Trent did the Pope wish to ratify? The Council had enacted penalties directly, i.e., the penal laws had their origin in its sessions, and indirectly, when the Fathers merely renewed the ancient discipline.

The question will immediately resolve itself, if one but considers the purpose of the constitution "*Apostolicae Sedis,*" which was to reduce the number of censures. If, then, the constitution ratified and renewed the penalties enacted indirectly by the Council of Trent, its purpose would have been defeated, for the maze of laws would have been as dense as ever. An examination of text itself will serve to illustrate the logic of this conclusion. The Council[173] had renewed in general terms the penalties against simony in benefices. If, therefore, the penalties ratified in a general way by the Council of Trent were to continue after the promulgation of the constitution, why did the Pope insert a special article[174] on this matter? The legislation regarding Papal elections as well as that which concerned the internal government of religious Orders were to remain in force. This applied to those laws which were functioning at the time of the constitution. Those which had fallen into desuetude, were not revived.[175]

---

[172] Pius IX, const. "*Apostolicae Sedis,*" 12 oct. 1869—*Fontes*, n. 552.

[173] Sess. XXIV, *de ref.*, c. 14.

[174] Const. "*Apostolicae Sedis,*" § II, n. 8.

[175] Smith, *Elements*, III, n. 3275.

α. *Benefices*

Those guilty of real simony in any kind of benefices whatsoever, together with their accomplices, were to incur excommunication reserved to the Roman Pontiff.[176] The same censure was incurred by those guilty of confidential simony, but in the latter case, the words *cujuscumque dignitatis* were added.[177] Pius IV had inflicted interdict upon prelates and excommunication upon others. Pius V extended the excommunication to prelates, so that after his time, a double penalty of excommunication and interdict was incurred by prelates and cardinals. The interdict was abolished by the silence of the present constitution on this point, but the excommunication as set forth by Pius V was ratified by Pius IX. The Constitution "*Apostolicae Sedis*" uses the word *mediatores,* where Paul II[178] employed *complices.* The latter word seems to have had a broader meaning.[179] Mediators are not mentioned in connection with confidential simony, and hence the usual argument is advanced, that if the Pontiff wished to include them, he should have mentioned them expressly as he did in the preceding paragraph.

β. *Ordination*

The inducements and opportunities for simony in ordinations had been reduced greatly, and Pius IX abrogated the censures attached to such crimes by omitting them from the constitution. Although the Council of Trent did issue a decree against simony in ordinations,[180] the enactment was merely a ratification of the general legislation which had been made in former times. Hence such a general and indirect ratification did not remain in force.[181] The suspension from the hope of receiving higher orders continued after the promulgation of the constitution, since this was rather an irregularity and not a censure.

---

[176] Const. "*Apostolicae Sedis,*" § II, n. 8.

[177] *Loc. cit.*, n. 9.

[178] C. 2, *de simonia,* V, 1, in Extravag. com.

[179] *Nouvelle Revue Théologique,* IX (1887), 368.

[180] Sess. XXI, *de ref.*, c. 1.

[181] Wernz, *Jus Decretalium,* VI, n. 342; Leech, *A Comparative Study,* p. 149.

γ. *Entrance to Religion*

Those guilty of simony in entrance to religion incur also excommunication reserved to the Holy See.[182] This does not apply to the charging for the sustenance of novices, which was permitted by the Council of Trent,[183] nor to the dowry which nuns were obliged to demand from entrants.

δ. *Indulgences*

Those who trafficked in indulgences or other spiritual favors were to incur excommunication according to the provisions of the constitution *"Quam plenum,"*[184] of Pius V. Pius V had laid down this penalty for the inferiors of bishops, and the commentators on the present constitution concluded that the penalty here should not extend beyond these limits.[185] The interdict formerly incurred by bishops, Cardinals and other dignitaries, was abrogated. Among the spiritual favors which had been subject to abuse might be mentioned, the granting of permission, for a sum of money, to choose a confessor who might absolve from all censures, the publication or concession of indulgences for money, the permission to offer the Holy Sacrifice or to grant Christian burial, the permission to eat meat on days of abstinence, the permission to have more sponsors at Baptism than were allowed by the Council of Trent,[186] and absolution from a censure incurred by simony.[187]

ε. *Traffic in Mass Stipends*

In condemning a contrary proposition, Alexander VII[188] launched an attack upon an abuse which, in spite of the severe

---

[182] Const. *"Apostolicae Sedis,"* § 10—Fontes, n. 552.

[183] Sess. XXIV, *de regularibus*, c. 16.

[184] 2 jan. 1569—*Fontes*, n. 132. The entire text of this constitution is not given in the *Fontes*. Cf. *Bullarium Romanum*, tom. IV, sect. III, p. 91.

[185] Pennachi, *Commentarium* in const. "Apostolicae Sedis," I, 934-935.

[186] Sess. XXIV, *de ref. matrim.*, c. 2.

[187] Const. *"Quam plenum,"* § 1-3. These spiritual favors are not contained in the *Fontes*; cf. *Bullarium Romanum, loc. cit.*

[188] Prop. IX, damn. ab Alex. VII—Denziger, *Enchiridion*, n. 980.

penalties attached to it, was to continue even to our own time. The cause was sponsored also by Innocent XII[189], who declared that the practice of transferring masses to other priests at a lower stipend was to be abolished. Benedict XIV[190] added the penalty of excommunication for a lay person and suspension for clerics, both censures being reserved to the Holy See. These penalties were to be incurred by those who collected mass stipends for the purpose of transferring them after retaining part of the stipend. Pius IX[191] extended the excommunication to all guilty persons, whether cleric or lay, but the suspension was abrogated by the silence of the Pontiff on this point.

Notwithstanding the penalties attached to such abuses, the vice continued. Booksellers and merchants continued to organize public collections of stipends and retained the money as payment for books, wine or other merchandise. The warning of the Sacred Congregation of the Council,[192] of July 25, 1874, had very little effect. In the decree "*Vigilanti,*"[193] there seems to have been a relaxation of the severe discipline of Pius IX. Clerics in major orders were to incur suspension *a divinis*, other clerics, irregularity, and laics excommunication, all censures and penalties being reserved to the Ordinary. The law was later extended to the Eastern Church[194] and confirmed by a later decree of the Sacred Congregation of the Council.[195]

The place where the masses were said did not alter the case. The words of the constitution "*Apostolicae Sedis,*" " . . . in locis ubi Missarum stipendia minoris pretii esse solent," gave rise to the doubt whether the censure would be incurred if the stipends were kept in the same region where they were received, but said by a priest for a smaller stipend. The question was

---

189 Const. "*Nuper,*" 23 dec. 1679—*Fontes,* n. 260.

190 Encycl. "*Quanta cura,*" 30 jun. 1741—*Fontes,* n. 311.

191 Const. "*Apostolicae Sedis,*" § 12—*Fontes,* n. 552; cf. Leech, *A Comparative Study,* p. 67.

192 *ASS,* VIII (1874), 107.

193 S.C.C., decr. "*Vigilanti,*" 25 maii 1893—*ASS,* XXVI (1893), 56-59.

194 S.C. de Prop. Fide, litt. encycl. (ad Ep. Orient.), 20 jan. 1893—*Collectanea,* n. 1847.

195 S.C.C., decr. "*Ut debita,*" 11 maii 1904—*ASS,* XXXVI (1904), 672; cf. Leech, *op. cit.,* 85.

placed before the Sacred Congregation of the Holy Office,[196] "Whether those who collected stipends for masses to be said in the same locality, where the money was collected, for a smaller stipend, incurred the censure?" The answer was given in the affirmative.

In some instances the Holy See has relaxed the stringent law on stipends by means of particular indults and responses. Thus Rome has reluctantly permitted a certain bishop to appoint an official collector of stipends whose commission was to be three per-cent of the amount collected.[197] In another case, the Sacred Congregation of the Council tolerated a practice whereby the pastor gave the curate the stipend customary for a low mass when he said a high mass, and kept the difference for his board and lodging.[198] While this is not the abuse which Pius IX had in mind, and while, too, the Church is free to change her own laws at will, it seems to be contrary to the spirit of the law upon the indivisibility of the stipend.

Essentially, the constitution "*Apostolicae Sedis*" remained the penal law of the Church until the promulgation of the Code. Many of its provisions were incorporated without change, some were changed substantially, while others were abolished. The law upon the election of the Sovereign Pontiff received its first modification in the constitution "*Vacante Sede Apostolica.*"[199] Simony was no longer considered an invalidating factor in the papal election.

---

[196] S.C. S. Off., 13 jan. 1892, ad 4—*Fontes*, n. 1147.

[197] S.C.C., 18 mar. 1905—*ASS*, XXXVIII (1905), 79; cf. Keller, *Mass Stipends*, p. 74.

[198] *ASS*, XXXVII (1904), 524; cf. also S.C.C., 26 feb. 1910, *AAS*, II (1910), 203.

[199] Pius X, const. "*Vacante Sede Apostolica,*" 25 dec. 1904—*Cod. Jur. Can.*, Doc. I.

PART II

PRESENT LEGISLATION

CHAPTER II

THE DEFINITION AND DIVISION OF SIMONY

Canon 727.—§ 1. Studiosa voluntas emendi vel vedendi pro pretio temporali rem intrinsece spiritualem, ex. gr., Sacramenta, ecclesiasticam jurisdictionem, consecrationem, indulgentias, etc., vel rem temporalem rei spirituali adnexam ita ut res temporalis sine spirituali nullo modo esse possit, ex. gr., beneficium ecclesiasticum, etc., aut res spiritualis sit objectum, etsi partiale, contractus, ex. gr., consecratio in calicis consecrati venditione, est simonia juris divini.

§ 2. Dare vero res temporales spirituali adnexas pro temporalibus spirituali adnexis, vel res spirituales pro spiritualibus, vel etiam temporales pro temporalibus, si id ob periculum irreverentiae erga res spirituales ab Ecclesia prohibeatur, est simonia juris ecclesiastici.

Canon 728.—Cum de simonia agitur, emptio-venditio, permutatio, etc., late accipiendae sunt pro qualibet conventione, licet ad effectum non deducta, etiam tacita, in qua scilicet animus simoniacus expresse non manifestetur, sed ex circumstantiis colligatur.

With perhaps the exception of ecclesiastical offices and admission to the religious state, the sacred things which had been the objects of abuse throughout the history of the Church have been gathered together in the Third Book of the Code. It is only logical, therefore, that at the very outset it should be stated definitely that such things are beyond the pale of commercialism. Accordingly, the codifiers inserted as a necessary preface to the treatment of ecclesiastical things several canons upon the nature and scope of simony.

Article I.—Simony of the Divine Law

Simony of the divine law[1] is a deliberate design of buying or selling for a temporal price, such things as are spiritual in themselves or annexed to spirituals; or of making the spiritual thing at least the partial object of the contract. With a few additional notes, necessary for the sake of clarity, the classic definition[2] has been embodied in the Code. In such transactions, spiritual things are measured in terms of temporal goods, when in reality they are beyond all wordly evaluation. Hence there is sufficient profanation of a sacred thing to constitute a real sacrilege.[3] In the definition accepted by authors before the Code, reference was made to simony of the divine law alone. The reason for this was probably because some theologians and canonists[4] held that what is called simony of the ecclesiastical law is not really simony since the temporal price is lacking.

Marianus Socinus[5] argued that the definition given by St. Thomas was inadequate, since it referred only to mental simony. To substantiate his opinion, he cited the *Gloss*[6] as adding the words *cum effectu*, in order to extend the definition to include external simony. But the *Gloss* takes rather the legal aspect of the question, designating such simony as might be proven and punished in the external forum. Considering the general aspects of simony, the word *voluntas* is even more correct than would be simply the terms *buying* or *selling*. The object of every sale should be a thing which can be appraised and must be at least

---

[1] The expression *divine law* refers here to the divine natural law which is written in the hearts of men, and not to the divine positive law as contained in revelation. Cf. Schmalzgrueber, *Jus Ecclesiasticum Universum,* lib. V, tit. III, n. 20; Suarez, *Opera Omnia,* tom. XIII, lib. IV, c. 2, n. 6.

[2] St. Thomas, *Summa Theologica,* 2, 2, q. 100, art. 1.

[3] Suarez, *Opera Omnia,* tom. XIII, lib. IV, c. 1, n. 7; Schmalzgrueber, *Jus Ecclesiasticum Universum,* lib. V, tit. III, n. 12; Ballerini-Palmieri, *Opus Theologicum Morale,* II, tr. VI, n. 219; Genicot, *Institutiones Theologiae Moralis,* I, n. 283.

[4] Laymann, *Theologia Moralis,* lib. IV, tr. X, c. 8, n. 66; Sotus, *De Justitia et Jure,* lib. IX, q. 5, art. 2.

[5] Quoted by Gonzalez, *Commentarium Perpetuum,* lib. V, tit. III, c. 1, n. 13.

[6] C. 1, C. I, q. 1.

the delegated property of the seller.[7] A spiritual thing, however, cannot be appraised, since it is beyond all earthly value; nor does it belong to men, for men are not the owners, but merely the custodians of spiritual goods. "Let a man so account of us as of the ministers of Christ and the dispensers of the mysteries of God," says St. Paul.[8] Hence the actual buying or selling of the spiritual object is impossible, and all that can be present is the attempt, the simulation, the will to buy or sell.[9] The same objection might be raised against the addition of terms to make the simoniacal will external. Such a definition would exclude purely mental simony, which authors sometimes distinguish, and would confine the description to those species of simony which are externally manifested.

§ 1. *The Deliberate Design*

The expression *studiosa voluntas*[10] emphasizes the fact that even though no explicit contract exists between the parties, there still may be simony involved.[11] The existence of a deliberate intention is sufficient for the commission of simony, but the very nature of the vice usually leads to an external expression. Canon Law considers simony only where there has been such a manifestation.[12] In the Code, therefore, the words imply not only the essential malice of a sin against the virtue of religion,

---

[7] The sale of the property of another without his consent would be invalid. Cf. Pruemmer, *Manuale Theologiae Moralis*, II, n. 242.

[8] I Cor., IV, 1.

[9] Pichler, *Jus Canonicum*, lib. V, tit. III, c. 1, n. 4; Gonzalez, *Commentarium Perpetuum*, lib. V, tit. III, c. 1, n. 13.

[10] The words *studiosa voluntas* are variously rendered in the vernacular by different authors: *serious endeavor* (Koch-Preuss, *Moral Theology*, IV, 235; Slater, *Manual of Moral Theology*, I, 231); *intentional will* (Woywod, *New Canon Law*, n. 570); *deliberate design* (Weber, *History of Simony*, p. 2); *deliberate eagerness* (Augustine, *A Commentary on Canon Law*, IV, 6); *studious intention* (Ayrinhac, *Penal Legislation*, p. 329).

[11] Laymann, *Theologia Moralis*, tom. I, lib. IV, tr. 10, c. 8, n. 1; Slater, *loc. cit.*; Schmalzgrueber, *Jus Ecclesiasticum Universum*, lib. V, tit. III, n. 73.

[12] Augustine, *A Commentary*, IV, 6; Deshayes, *Memento Juris Ecclesiastici Publici*, n. 1996.

but the juridical element of manifestation. Reiffenstuel[13] demands the existence of a contract. Essentially, however, no express pact is required.[14] It is sufficient that there be a simoniacal affection on the part of one of the parties and the action follow. For while simony usually involves complicity, there can be no doubt that guilt is incurred when one of the parties intends the transaction, e.g., when a cleric serves a prelate without salary with the intention of obligating him to confer a benefice.[15]

There must be present the intention of obligating someone. Hence there would be no simony if the spiritual object were given only in the hope of receiving a temporal reward.[16] Such a state of mind is far different from that which would prompt one to give something for the sole purpose of placing another under obligation. The attitude of the automobilist who invited a chance acquaintance to ride with him, hoping that the stranger would help defray the expenses of the trip, would be quite different from that of a taxi-driver who offered his machine for the same journey. In the first instance the passenger is not bound to reimburse his host, while in the latter case, he is placed under a strict obligation to pay the charges. This hope of recompense may even be manifested, since such a manifestation places no obligation upon the recipient of the favor. Whatever is licit to hope for, is licit to express.[17]

The hope of recompense must be carefully distinguished from the state of mind by which one gives something temporal, not as a price, but as a motive for obtaining something spiritual, or with the intention of binding another to gratuitous com-

---

[13] *Jus Canonicum Universum,* lib. V, tit. III, n. 63.

[14] Can. 728.

[15] Schmalzgrueber, *Jus Ecclesiasticum Universum,* lib. V, tit. III, n. 48; De Meester, *Compendium,* III, n. 1098; Leinz, *Die Simonie,* pp. 46, 47; Farrugia, *Commentarium,* p. 98, a.

[16] Vermeersch-Creusen, *Epitome,* II, n. 3; Pichler, *Jus Canonicum,* lib. V, tit. III, n. 29; Suarez, *Opera Omnia,* tom. XIII, lib. IV, tr. 10, c. 45, nn. 4-6.

[17] Noldin, *Summa Theologiae Moralis,* II, n. 181; Pichler, *Jus Canonicum,* lib. V, tit. III, c. 3, n. 28.

pensation.[18] In the former case, what was called motive, is really the price, hence the donation is not entirely gratuitous, even though it may be called so.[19] If the donor had not the intention of obligating the recipient to return some spiritual favor, he would not have presented the gift, and if he does not receive what he seeks, he considers himself cheated.[20] Innocent XI condemned the proposition which vindicated of simony those who bestowed spiritual favors as a motive for impelling others to return some temporal good, or under guise of just remuneration. In these condemned theses it was supposed that the temporal was given for the spiritual with at least an implicit contract or agreement. There would be simony even if the object of the pact were due the person from the natural obligation of gratitude, for the contract adds a new obligation.[21]

In considering the prohibition of contracts or agreements concerning the natural obligation of gratuitous compensation, it seems that the law must be interpreted as forbidding the binding of the recipient to the expression of gratitude in a determined way. The donor could oblige in an express contract to gratitude in general, because he thereby does not impose a new obligation distinct from the duty arising from the natural law. However, to demand gratitude in a stipulated manner or to a given amount, would undoubtedly be simoniacal.[22] But there would be no simony involved where the compensation was purely gratuitous, without any agreement on the part of the persons

---

[18] Augustine, *A Commentary,* IV, 6; Ballerini-Palmieri, *Opus Theologicum Morale,* II, tr. VI, n. 220; Denzinger, *Enchiridion,* nn. 1062, 1063.

[19] St. Alphonsus, *Theologia Moralis,* lib. III, n. 54.

[20] Schmalzgrueber, *Jus Ecclesiasticum Universum,* lib. V, tit. III, n. 73.

[21] Schmalzgrueber, *Jus Ecclesiasticum Universum,* lib. V, tit. III, n. 62; Gibalinus, *De Simonia,* q. 10, c. 3, n. 5; Suarez, *Opera Omnia,* tom. XIII, lib. IV, c. 45, n. 11; Laymann, *Theologia Moralis,* tom. I, lib. IV, tr. 10, c. 8, n. 9. Pichler (*Jus Canonicum,* lib. V, tit. III, c. 3, n. 29) illustrates this by describing the case of a man who refused to sell his horse to a friend, because he considered it a breach of hospitality and friendship to charge for the animal. Accordingly he gave the horse to the man with the understanding that, out of gratitude, his friend would give him 100 gold pieces.

[22] Pichler, *Jus Canonicum,* lib. V, tit. III, c. 3, n. 29.

concerned as to the manner or the amount, for to remunerate a gift is not to buy it.[23]

§ 2. *Buying or Selling*

When there is question of simony, the terms "purchase," "sale" and other similar expressions are to be taken in a wide sense, as including any stipulation, even though not fulfilled, or made in a tacit manner. In the latter case, though the simoniacal intention were not explicitly manifested, it could be gathered from the circumstances.[24] If in return for a sum of money, a bishop would promise to ordain a candidate, there would be an express pact between the parties. On the other hand, if a cleric who was not noted for his generosity, would give a sum of money to a prelate, when he heard that a parish was vacant, and the bishop in turn would appoint him to the parish, it could be presumed from the circumstances that a tacit contract existed.[25] Leinz[26] took exception to the definition given by St. Thomas. Only the acts of buying or selling are mentioned therein, whereas any contract, or legally binding transaction, in which the exchange of these objects takes place, is sufficient to constitute simony. Pruemmer[27] undertakes to answer this objection by calling attention to the fact that the definition has been adopted by the Code.[28] But the Code did not adopt the definition because it was exhaustive and complete. Probably because it was the definition accepted by Theologians and Canonists for centuries, and was regarded as classic, it was embodied in the law. On the contrary, rather than refuting the objection of Leinz, the law seems to have taken cognizance of it, by tacitly admitting the inadequacy of the definition of simony. Since canon 727 does not entirely cover the case, canon 728 was inserted to explain that the terms of purchase and sale

[23] Suarez, *Opera Omnia*, tom. XIII, lib. IV, c. 45, nn. 4-6.
[24] Can. 728. Cf. Augustine, *A Commentary*, IV, 7.
[25] Pichler, *Jus Canonicum*, lib. V, tit. III, c. 3, n. 28.
[26] *Die Simonie*, p. 40; *Ak KR*, LXXVII (1897), 267-272.
[27] *Manuale Theologiae Moralis*, II, n. 555.
[28] Can. 727, § 1.

are to be understood in a wide rather than a restricted sense. Hence all onerous contracts are included.[29]

Alexander III gave a practical test to determine whether the transfer of goods might be considered as purely gratuitous, or as a price paid for the spiritual thing.[30] Three things must be examined: 1. The quality of the donor, for if he were a relative or a very close friend, the presumption would be in favor of the gratuity of the gift; 2. The quality of the gift; if it were absolutely or relatively moderate, the donation might be considered gratuitous, while on the other hand, a considerable sum might arouse suspicion about the intention of the giver; 3. The time of the presentation; if the gift preceded or followed the conferring of the spiritual favor by a long space of time, the presumption would be in favor of the purity of intention; whereas the contrary would be true, if both actions were closely allied.

§ 3. *The Temporal Price*

Some authors believe that the phrase *pretio temporali* is superfluous, since the terms *buying* and *selling* involve the notion of price.[31] In its strictest sense, the word *price* would mean the value of a thing expressed in terms of money, but in a broader sense it signifies the value of a thing expressed in terms of other things of value.[32] The meaning of temporal price was fully described by Gregory the Great. He mentioned three species of price which he termed *munus a manu, munus a lingua* and *munus ab obsequio,* and his terminology has been preserved in Moral Theology and Canon Law.[33] By the word *munus,* he meant anything which would induce an obligation from commutative justice, hence excluding all purely gratuitous gifts, albeit they induce an obligation from the natural law.[34]

---

[29] Vermeersch-Creusen, *Epitome,* II, n. 5; Gibalinus, *De Simonia,* q. I, n. 1; *Il Monitore Ecclesiastico,* I (1919), 40.

[30] C. 18, X, *de simonia,* V, 3.

[31] Pichler, *Jus Canonicum,* lib. V, tit. III, c. 3, n. 3; Gibalinus, *De Simonia,* q. I, n. 1.

[32] Vermeersch-Creusen, *Epitome,* II, n. 5.

[33] "Munus quippe ab obsequio est subjectio indebite impensa. Munus a manu, pecunia est; munus a lingua, favor."—c. 114, C. I, q. 1.

[34] Ballerini-Palmieri, *Opus Theologicum Morale,* II, tr. VI, n. 221.

i. *The Munus a Manu*

The *munus a manu* is generally understood to mean money paid for a spiritual object, though it might embrace also other material things, such as a palace, an automobile, etc. The term might include even rights or privileges, since these also have their value.[35] The cancellation of a debt in return for some spiritual gift would also fall within the scope of the *munus a manu.*[36]

ii. *The Munus a Lingua*

The *munus a lingua* comprises oral commendation, public expression of approval, moral support in high places, adulation, flattery of a kind which is a matter of stipulation, and therefore procures a benefit.[37] The same condition would be present if the grantor acquiesced to the wishes of the petitioner because he did not wish to offend him. In this case, the good will of the recipient would be the price received for the spiritual gift. The *munus a lingua* would embrace also the case of a person who refused to grant a spiritual favor unless asked by a certain dignitary, whom he wishes to place under obligation, e.g., I shall not grant the benefice unless the Archbishop requests me to do it.[38] This is a constituent element of the most insidious kind of simony, and one which could flourish without attracting much attention.

Suarez indicates how the term *munus a lingua* is carried too far by some authors and extended to include not only any favor of the tongue which might be sought, but also the supplications

---

[35] Santi, *Praelectiones Juris Canonici,* lib. V, tit. III, n. 3; Ballerini-Palmieri, *loc. cit.,* n. 222; St. Thomas, *Summa Theologica,* 2, 2, q. 100, art. 5.

[36] "Si quis obligatione liberatus sit, potest videri accepisse."—Dig. 115, 50, 17.

[37] Augustine, *A Commentary,* IV, 8; Weber, *History,* p. 4; Santi, *Praelectiones Juris Canonici,* lib. V, tit. III, n. 3; Ballerini-Palmieri, *Opus Theologiae Moralis,* II, tr. VI, n. 231.

[38] Schmalzgrueber, *Jus Ecclesiasticum Universum,* lib. V, tit. III, n. 114; Suarez, *Opera Omnia,* tom. XIII, lib. IV, c. 40, n. 13; Scavini, *Opus Theologicum,* II, tr. V, diss. II, c. 2, n. 2.

which a person makes in behalf of himself or another.[39] They cite as their authority St. Thomas Aquinas.[40] "Oral remuneration," says the Angelic Doctor, "denotes either praise that pertains to human favor, which has its price, or a request whereby man's favor is obtained, or the contrary is avoided. Hence if one intend this chiefly, one commits simony. Now to grant a request made for an unworthy person, implies, seemingly, that this is one's chief intention, wherefore the deed itself is simoniacal. But if the request is made for a worthy person, the deed itself is not simoniacal, because it is based on a worthy cause, on account of which a spiritual thing is granted to the person for whom the request is made. Nevertheless there may be simony in the intention, if one look, not to the worthiness of the person, but to the human favor. If, however, a person asks for himself, that he may obtain the cure of souls, his very presumption renders him unworthy, and so his request is made for an unworthy person. But if one be in need, one may lawfully seek for oneself an ecclesiastical benefice without the cure of souls."

An analysis of the text will suffice to convince one that the argument condemning one's own supplications as simoniacal, is unjustly attributed to St. Thomas. He plainly speaks of one who is seeking human favor. His conjectures on the worthiness of the person for whom the favor is asked, are merely attempts to formulate a rule whereby the intention of the person asking can be judged. If, for example, the person for whom the favor is asked, has no merits of his own to recommend him, then manifestly the person who asks for him, hopes to use his own influence to secure the favor. It is the thought that the grantor will not want to offend the person asking, which prompts the action. St. Thomas admits that if the person is worthy, there is no simony. In this case, the recipient hopes to secure the benefice upon his own merits, not through the influence of the one who petitions for him.[41] If the word *munus* is considered in the

---

[39] *Opera Omnia*, tom. XIII, lib. IV, c. 40, nn. 1-11.

[40] *Summa Theologica*, 2, 2, q. 100, art. 5, ad 3.

[41] "Unde D. Thom. 2, 2, q. 100, a. 5, ad 3, licet dicat, non esse licitum pro se petere beneficium, curam animarum habens, vel episcopatum, propter

sense of remuneration, the case will resolve itself immediately. A person who makes supplication in his own behalf or for another certainly does not offer any remuneration by his petition.

While it would not be simoniacal to ask another to intercede for him,[42] a person could not pay for this intercession without being guilty of simony, unless the money were given for the labor connected with the making of the petition, or for the inconvenience suffered thereby.[43] Such intercession would be the moral cause of the granting of the spiritual favor, and whoever purchases this, may be considered as having bought the spiritual thing itself.[44] It makes little difference that the intercessions themselves are something temporal, because they become virtually spiritual because of their close connection with the spiritual.[45]

It would not be simoniacal to pay someone to manifest a candidate's merits to the superior or to secure for him a necessary audience with the proper authorities, for such actions cannot be called the moral cause of the granting of the favor. What really moves the superior is the talents of the candidate, and the manifestation of them or the audience is only remotely

---

praesumptionem, si se reputet dignum, vel propter injustitiam si se reputet indignum, non tamen dicit esse simoniam, quod illi falso imponit Sylvester.''—Suarez, *Opera Omnia*, tom. XIII, lib. IV, c. 40, n. 5.

[42] Pichler, *Jus Canonicum*, lib. V, tit. III, c. 3, n. 25; Suarez, *Opera Omnia*, tom. XIII, lib. IV, c. 40, n. 9.

[43] St. Alphonsus, *Theologia Moralis*, lib. III, n. 64; Schmalzgrueber, *Jus Ecclesiasticum Universum*, lib. V, tit. III, n. 102; Navarrus, *Manuale*, c. 23, n. 106; Lessius, *De Justitia et Jure*, lib. II, c. 35, n. 46; Suarez, *Opera Omnia*, tom. XIII, lib. IV, c. 53, n. 14.

[44] Schmalzgrueber, *Jus Ecclesiasticum Universum*, lib. V, tit. III, n. 102; Suarez, *loc. cit.*, n. 15.

[45] Ballerini-Palmieri (*Opus Theologicum Morale*, II, tr. VI, nn. 235-240) take the opposite view. They argue that since the granting of the spiritual favor is gratuitous, the moral cause is not to be impugned. Certainly if one who makes intercession for another places the moral cause of the granting of the favor, why cannot the same be said concerning one who merely manifests a person's merits, or secures him an audience? Cf. Gennari, *Consultazioni*, I, n. 93; Noldin, *Summa Theologiae Moralis*, II, n. 188.

connected with the actual spiritual good.[46] In practice, however, it is usually difficult to determine whether the money has been paid simply for the manifestation of merits or for intercession. There is always danger that the mediator will exaggerate the candidate's merits, especially if the gift were a large one.[47]

iii. *The Munus ab Obsequio*

The *munus ab obsequio* involves service of any kind, either actual or habitual, not due by reason of mutual obligation, but rendered with a view to obtaining a spiritual favor.[48] Here again, it must be noted that free and voluntary service rendered to the grantor, even though in the hope of obtaining the spiritual object, is not to be considered as the price paid for the supernatural and hence simoniacal. Of course, there may be grounds for suspicion in such cases. Hence, any demonstration of undue subjection and the rendering of service not demanded by some obligation, might furnish the occasion for calling into doubt the intention of the person performing the actions.[49] Thus if a bishop appointed a priest to a parish on condition that he would act as his secretary without salary, he would be guilty of simony *ratione muneris ab obsequio*.[50]

§ 4. *The Spiritual Object*

The spiritual object in a simoniacal transaction is usually called the *merx spiritualis*, or the merchandise, so to speak, which is bought or sold. This can be either intrinsically spiritual, that is spiritual by its very nature, or it can be a temporal thing which is united to a spiritual object.

---

[46] Schmalzgrueber, *Jus Ecclesiasticum Universum*, lib. V, tit. III, n. 104; Suarez, *Opera Omnia*, tom. XIII, lib. IV, c. 53, n. 17; Alphonsus, *Theologia Moralis*, lib. III, n. 64.

[47] Reiffenstuel, *Jus Canonicum Universum*, lib. V, tit. III, n. 125.

[48] Ballerini-Palmieri, *Opus Theologicum Morale*, II, tr. VI, n. 242; Santi, *Praelectiones Juris Canonici*, lib. V, tit. III, n. 3; Vermeersch-Creusen, *Epitome*, II, n. 5.

[49] Weber, *A History*, p. 4; Augustine, *A Commentary*, IV, 9.

[50] St. Alphonsus, *Theologia Moralis*, lib. III, n. 64.

i. *Intrinsically Spiritual Objects*

Leinz[51] contends that the words employed here are too comprehensive; for in simony there is involved only a certain class of spiritual things. The natural knowledge of the human mind is undoubtedly spiritual, yet it does not come within the scope of simony. He prefers the word *supernatural.* However, the term is used in its more restricted sense and signifies any object which, by the institution of God or of the Church, pertains to eternal salvation or the means of attaining it.[52] Hence, sanctifying grace, actual grace, the sacraments, the sacramentals, the power of orders, dispensations, absolutions, jurisdiction, all are embraced by the term *spiritual object.*[53] Some things are *formaliter* destined for the salvation of souls, i.e., in themselves and by their very nature, as for example, sanctifying grace; others are *causaliter,* in so far as they are the causes of spiritual things, as the sacraments, sermons, prayers and the sacramentals; while others are *effective* related to salvation, in as much as they proceed from a spiritual cause, or through the exercise of a spiritual faculty, as dispensations, absolution, consecration, blessings, presentation, confirmation and conferring of benefices, and other acts of ecclesiastical jurisdiction.[54]

ii. *Annexed to Spiritual Objects*

Temporal things may be annexed to a spiritual object in one of three ways: 1. *Antecedently,* that is when the temporal object existed before, and the spiritual character is added to it. Such would be all consecrated things, the material out of which they are made having existed before the blessing or consecration

[51] *Die Simonie,* p. 40.

[52] Schmalzgrueber, *Jus Ecclesiasticum Universum,* lib. V, tit. III, n. 153; Reiffenstuel, *Jus Canonicum Universum,* lib. V, tit. III, n. 44; Weber, *A History,* p. 5; Noldin, *Summa Theologiae Moralis,* II, 183; Scavini, *Theologia Moralis,* II, n. 147.

[53] Pruemmer, *Manuale Theologiae Moralis,* II, n. 556; Bonacina, *Opera Omnia,* tom. I, q. 4, n. 10, 8o; q. 6, n. 17, 3io.

[54] C. 24, 36, 39, X *de simonia,* V, 3; Scavini, *Theologia Moralis,* II, n. 147; Alphonsus, *Theologia Moralis,* lib. III, n. 49; Genicot, *Institutiones Theologiae Moralis,* I, n. 283.

was attached. 2. *Concomitantly,* if the spiritual object begins to exist at the same time as the temporal thing. Concomitant annexation may be either *extrinsic,* if it is merely accidental and can be dissolved, e.g., the chanting at High Mass, the journey to administer the Sacraments; or *intrinsic,* if it is essential and indissoluble, as the labor connected with the administration of the sacraments, or the fatigue which of necessity must accompany any spiritual exercise. 3. *Consequently,* if the temporal thing follows or is derived from the spiritual, e.g., the revenues connected with a benefice.

The Code speaks of a two-fold connection of the temporal with the spiritual: 1. *essential or necessary,* when the temporal is so intimately joined to the spiritual, that without it, the temporal could not exist, as a benefice; 2. *antecedent or concomitant extrinsic,* when the temporal retains its own value, as the gold in a chalice.[55] It matters little whether the spiritual element is of strictly divine origin or of ecclesiastical institution, so long as it is spiritual in itself and attached to the temporal object by lawful authority.[56] Antecedent temporal goods still retain their intrinsic value and hence it is lawful to sell what is antecedently annexed to something spiritual, provided there is no negotiation concerning the spiritual character, and provided such a transaction has not been forbidden by the Church.[57] The extrinsic labor or inconvenience connected with the saying of mass at a late hour, or the administration of the sacraments at a distant place, has its negotiable value, and hence might be compensated without danger of simony of the divine law. However, the prescriptions of the ecclesiastical law must also be considered. The controversy concerning the morality of charging for the intrinsic labor connected with the celebration of

[55] Cans. 727, § 1 and 730.

[56] Augustine, *A Commentary,* IV, 11.

[57] Thus it would not be simony to sell consecrated chalices, indulgenced rosaries or medals, sepulchres of relics, provided the price is not increased on account of their spiritual character.—Can. 1539, § 1. However, when rosaries are sold, the indulgences attached to them are lost.—Can. 924, § 2. Though the containers in which relics are sealed may be sold for their extrinsic value, it is absolutely forbidden to sell the relics themselves.—Can. 1289.

mass or the administration of the sacraments seems to have been settled definitely by the Code. The value of the labor arises from its intimate connection with spiritual things, and has no worth apart from its spiritual character. Canon 727, § 1, expressly states that to sell a temporal thing which cannot exist apart from the spiritual, is simony of the divine law.[58]

ARTICLE II.—SIMONY OF THE ECCLESIASTICAL LAW

The Church had placed her sanction upon the divine law, and had attached to the violation of it the most severe penalties. She went beyond this legislation, however, and as a consequence, there is simony of purely ecclesiastical law. There are some actions which, although they do not constitute a comparison between the spiritual and the temporal and the consequent reduction of the former to the level of the latter, nevertheless might lead to simony of the divine law. Accordingly ecclesiastical authority forbids at times and under certain circumstances the exchange of one spiritual thing for another or temporal objects annexed to spiritual things for other temporal objects of the same character, or even temporal objects for other temporal objects, when in such transactions there might be danger of irreverence or grave abuse. Thus the malice of the exchange of benefices upon private authority arises solely from the prohibition of the Church, and must be considered simony of the ecclesiastical law. The lawfulness of the exchange of benefices depends upon the approbation of the Ordinary, and if simony of the divine law were involved, such approbation could not legalize the action. The obligation of guarding against abuses devolves upon the Ordinary of the place.[59]

Simony of the ecclesiastical law embraces the charging for testimonial letters,[60] fees for admission to the church for divine

[58] Cf. Noldin, *Summa Theologiae Moralis*, II, n. 184, 2o; Maurer, "Arbeitslohn und Honorar für sündhafte Handlungen," *Zeitschrifft für Kath. Theologie*, XXXIII (1909), 480 ff.; Arendt, *De Laesione Justitiae Commutativae in Missae Manualis Stipendio Alteri Celebranti Diminuto*, (Prati, 1914), pp. 44-55.

[59] Can. 1261.

[60] Can. 545, § 1.

services,[61] traffic in Mass stipends, and the demanding more than is allowed by diocesan statute or legitimate custom for the administration of the sacraments.[62] The selling of relics according to some[63] must be considered simony of the ecclesiastical law, while others[64] contend, and it would seem rightly, that such transactions involve simony of the divine law, since their value depends upon their close connection with the spiritual.

There are some[65] who would claim that actions forbidden by the ecclesiastical law are not simony in the strict sense of the term, because there is lacking the essential comparison between the spiritual and the temporal. Durandus[66] argues that if such actions are wrong only because prohibited, then simony of the ecclesiastical law would be more a sin of disobedience than simony strictly so called. The prohibition of the Church would be sufficient to make them sinful, but not simoniacal, and some think that the law endorses this opinion by the addition of the words *ob periculum irreverentiae.*[67] However, when the Church proscribes morally indifferent actions from a motive of any virtue, she makes them the object of that virtue. Thus, before the enactment of the law concerning the Eucharistic fast, the reception of communion by one not fasting was not sinful. In view of the present precept, such an action would be irreverent and sacrilegious, outside of the danger of death. By ecclesiastical law, the morally indifferent action of fasting has become the object of the virtue of religion and any violation of this law is a sacrilege. So too, the Church has proscribed certain actions which in themselves are morally indifferent and has branded them as simoniacal. Hence, the common and more probable opinion is that actions forbidden by the Church on

---

[61] Can. 1181.

[62] Cans. 827, 736, 2324, 2408.

[63] Genicot, *Institutiones Theologiae Moralis,* I, 289, 3o; Pruemmer, *Manuale Theologiae Moralis,* II, n. 564, 6o.

[64] De Meester, *Compendium,* III, n. 1100, 1o; Cocchi, *Commentarium,* lib. III, pars III, tit. XVI, n. 116, b.

[65] Laymann, *Theologia Moralis,* lib. IV, tr. X, c. 8, n. 66; Pirhing, *Jus Canonicum,* lib. V, tit. III, n. 6; Sotus, *De Justitia,* lib. IX, q. 5, art. 2.

[66] *Speculum,* lib. IV, dist. XXV, q. 5, n. 9.

[67] Augustine, *A Commentary,* IV, 12.

account of the danger of irreverence become simoniacal because of the prohibition placed upon them.[68] The law against simony of the ecclesiastical dispensation, however, partakes of the same characteristics as any other ecclesiastical law, and may cease to bind under the same circumstances as the others.[69]

Article III.—The Divisions of Simony

Both simony of the divine law and simony of the ecclesiastical law are divided into *mental, conventional* and *real,* according to the degree of evolution of the act. Mental simony is the internal will or proposition by which, when one gives[70] a temporal thing to another, he intends to bind the recipient to grant a spiritual favor or *vice versa.* Thus a cleric would be guilty of mental simony if he were to give his bishop a sum of money or offer to serve him without salary, with the intention of obligating him to confer a parish upon him. This species is called mental, not because it consists in the bare mental intention, but because, even though there is an external manifestation, no contract exists between the parties. Some authors distinguish a form of simony which they call *purely mental.* This consists in the mere desire to commit simony, to buy or sell a spiritual thing, without any consequent external action. Mental simony

---

[68] Schmalzgrueber, *Jus Ecclesiasticum Universum,* lib. V, tit. III, nn. 23, 25; Suarez, *Opera Omnia,* tom. XIII, lib. IV, c. 2, n. 1; c. 7, n. 2; St. Alphonsus, *Theologia Moralis,* lib. III, n. 69; Lessius, *De Justitia et Jure,* lib. II, c. 35, n. 25; Reiffenstuel, *Jus Canonicum Universum,* lib. V, tit. III, n. 26; Ferreres, *Institutiones Canonicae,* II, n. 12; Wernz, *Jus Decretalium,* VI, n. 341; Genicot, *Institutiones Theologiae Moralis,* I, n. 284; Pruemmer, *Manuale Theologiae Moralis,* II, n. 558; Farrugia, *Commentarium,* n. 138.

[69] Cappello, *De Censuris,* n. 358; Genicot, *Institutiones Theologiae Moralis,* I, n. 284.

[70] Note that mental simony is defined as *when one gives,* for it is necessary that the internal affection be followed by the external action, in order to come within the scope of Canon Law. Although before God one commits simony at the precise moment when he internally proposes to buy or sell a spiritual thing, even though the intention is never carried to its effect, nevertheless such a disposition is rather internal simony than mental in the sense of the Canonists. Cf. Reiffenstuel, *Jus Canonicum Universum,* lib. V, tit. III, n. 15.

accompanied by external action, they call *mixed mental.*[71] It is not necessary that the simoniacal intention be present in the minds of both parties. It is sufficient for the party who places the action to have such an intention.[72] Mental simony can be present in the act of recompensing a person for something which is due him in justice. This will present no difficulty, if one considers that in such a case the spiritual object is given in exchange for what one has already received and now owes to his creditor. In such a transaction, it is not necessary that the recipient even know or suspect the simoniacal intention of the other party, but in such circumstances only the person possessing the simoniacal will can be considered guilty of simony.[73]

Simony is conventional when there is a contract either express or tacit, of giving a temporal thing for a spiritual, or *vice versa.*[74] Conventional simony may be of two kinds, *purely conventional* or *mixed conventional.*[75] Purely conventional simony consists in the mutual agreement alone, neither part of the contract having been fulfilled. Conventional simony is called mixed, when the contract is at least partially fulfilled by one of the parties. The contract which causes mental simony to become conventional, may be made not only by words, express and direct, but also by obscure and indirect terms or even by motions of the head, etc. A simulated donation might also constitute conventional simony, as long as it can be judged from the circumstances that there was a contract. In this connection,

[71] Suarez, *Opera Omnia,* tom. XIII, lib. IV, c. 14, n. 13; Ferraris, v. *Simonia,* art. I, n. vii; Schmalzgrueber, *Jus Ecclesiasticum Universum,* lib. V, tit. III, n. 27.

[72] Ballerini-Palmieri, *Opus Theologicum Morale,* II, tr. VI, n. 249; Pichler, *Jus Canonicum,* lib. V, tit. III, c. 1, n. 5.

[73] Schmalzgrueber, *Jus Ecclesiasticum Universum,* lib. V, tit. III, n. 28.

[74] Navarrus, *Manuale,* c. 23, n. 104; Reiffenstuel, *Jus Canonicum Universum,* lib. V, tit. III, n. 15; Sanchez, *Consilia Moralia,* lib. II, c. 3, dub. 10, n. 106; Cardini, *Teologia Morali,* II, pp. 605, 606; Moneta, *Tract. de Distrib. Quotidianis,* p. II, q. 18, n. 5.

[75] Slater's (*Manual of Moral Theology,* I, 233) terminology is not precise. He refers to purely conventional and *partly* conventional simony. *Partly* conventional would suggest lesser perfection, while far from being less perfect, the reverse would seem to be true, since the contract has been executed partially.

however, it should be noted that a mere promise would not be sufficient to constitute conventional simony. It must assume the character of a contract by being accepted as binding by the party to whom the promise is made.

Simony is called *real* when the agreement is fulfilled by both parties. This species of simony is often called *complete.* It is not required that the contract be fulfilled in its entirety in order that real simony be present. It is sufficient that it be partially fulfilled by both parties, e.g., if a man made a contract to give $100 for a benefice and paid $50 upon receiving the benefice, he would commit real simony.[76] The same would be true if the person selling the benefice would give only the title papers of the property, or a bill of sale.[77]

Before the Code, controversy was quite marked concerning the exact moment when simony would pass from the category of conventional to that of real. Some authors,[78] while admitting only the presence of mixed conventional simony if the temporal price were paid and the spiritual object not yet conferred, nevertheless held that once the spiritual object had been transferred, real simony was present, even though there was no exchange of money. They based their conclusions upon certain texts of Canon Law which seemed to inflict punishment even when the temporal price was merely promised.[79] In the case where the spiritual object was actually given at a later date, there seems to have been little profit in such a controversy, for even though the simony remained mixed conventional for a long time, the penalties became retroactive, when both sides of the contract were fulfilled, and took effect from the moment the pact was

---

[76] Reiffenstuel, *Jus Canonicum Universum,* lib. V, tit. III, n. 22; Schmalzgrueber, *Jus Ecclesiasticum Universum,* lib. V, tit. III, n. 34.

[77] Pruemmer, *Manuale Theologiae Moralis,* II, n. 559.

[78] Salmanticenses, *Cursus Theologiae Moralis,* III, tr. XIX, c. 1, n. 18; Concina, *Theologia Christiana,* X (*de Extr. Unct. et Ordine*), 1, diss. 3, c. 3; Cajetanus, *Opuscula de Simonia,* q. 2; Dom Soto, *De Jure et Justitia,* IX, q. 8, art. 1.

[79] Cf. Schmalzgrueber, *Jus Ecclesiasticum Universum,* lib. V, tit. III, n. 247.

made.[80] Since the Code, penalties are incurred by conventional[81] as well as real simony, and consequently such a controversy is only of historical import.

A particular kind of conventional simony grew up around the conferring of benefices.[82] When an ecclesiastical benefice[83] is procured for a person with the agreement that he will either resign in favor of a third party to be designated by the benefactor, or in favor of the benefactor himself, or that he will divide with him the revenues accruing from the benefice, such transactions are called *confidential* simony. The term *confidential* signifies that the fulfillment of the agreement is dependent entirely upon the good will of the person for whom the benefice is procured. The agreement being illicit, was not enforceable by law.[84]

Authors usually distinguish four methods of conferring benefices with reservations which would constitute confidential simony.[85]

1. *Reservation of accession:* when one procures a benefice for another, with the understanding that at some future time he will resign in favor of a third party, or in favor of the benefactor himself. Thus if a bishop wished to confer a benefice upon a relative who at the time was ineligible because of the impediment of age or some temporary irregularity, he would procure it for another cleric, with the secret agreement that, when his relative would become free of the impediment or irregularity, the possessor would resign in favor of him.

---

[80] Schmalzgrueber, *loc. cit.*, n. 35; Reiffenstuel, *loc. cit.*, n. 23.

[81] Can. 728.

[82] Pius IV, const., "*Romanum Pontificem,*" 17 oct. 1564—*Fontes*, n. 106; Pius V, const., "*Intolerabilis,*" 1 jun. 1569—*Fontes*, n. 130.

[83] "Diximus beneficium ecclesiasticum: nam si eaedem conditiones confidentialiter verificantur in pensione vel alio jure ecclesiastico procurando, esset utique casus simoniae communis, non autem confidentialis."—Santi, *Praelectiones Juris Canonici*, lib. V, tit. III, n. 11.

[84] Can. 729. Cf. Pruemmer, *Manuale Theologiae Moralis*, II, n. 559, not. 4.

[85] Schmalzgrueber, *Jus Ecclesiasticum Universum*, lib. V, tit. III, n. 38-40; Wernz, *Jus Decretalium*, VI, n. 341; Reiffenstuel, *Jus Canonicum Universum*, lib. V, tit. III, n. 42.

2. *Reservation of ingress:* when one is appointed to a benefice legitimately, but before taking possession of it, cedes it to another, on condition that he might regain it, should any circumstance arise which might prevent its retention by the other party. Thus a parochial benefice was conferred on Father Peter, but before taking possession of it, he transferred it to Father Paul, with the agreement that, if Father Paul were given a parish of his own, Father Peter would then take possession of his own parish.

3. *Reservation of regress:* when one resigns a benefice of which he has already taken possession, in favor of another person, on condition that at some future time, the new possessor will return it, if he should become incapable of retaining it. Thus, in the example given above, if Father Peter had already occupied his parish before resigning it to Father Paul, the confidential simony would have been by reservation of regress.

4. *Reservation of pension or part of the fruits of the benefice.* Authors before the Code were not agreed whether this species of simony constituted confidential simony, or merely conventional or real simony, depending on the fulfilment or nonfulfillment of the contract.[86] The Code has put an end to this controversy by declaring that benefices must be conferred without diminution and by condemning all deductions or reservations of beneficial fruits as common or unqualified simony.[87]

Ballerini[88] points out the reasons why the Church was so solicitous in stamping out confidence in benefices. In many

---

[86] Schmalzgrueber, (*Jus Ecclesiasticum Universum,* lib. V, tit. III, nn. 38-40), Reiffenstuel, (*Jus Canonicum Universum,* lib. V, tit. III, n. 42), Suarez, (*Opera Omnia,* tom. XIII, lib. IV, c. 43, nn. 7, 8), La Croix, (*Theologia Moralis,* lib. III, p. I, n. 66), Wernz, (*Jus Decretalium,* VI, n. 341), held that such a reservation would come under the heading of confidential simony. Navarrus, (*Consilia,* lib. V, *de simonia,* c. 76, n. 6) and Lessius (*De Justitia et Jure,* lib. II, c. 35, n. 97) defend the opinion that, if the reservation is made in favor of the one who granted the benefice or transferred it, only common simony would be committed; but if the reservation was for a third party, the simony would be confidential.

[87] Can. 1440-1441.

[88] *Opus Theologicum Morale,* II, tr. VI, n. 261; cf. Conc. Trident., sess. XXV, *de ref.,* c. 7.

cases the return of the benefice to its original possessor, or the one to whom it was granted legitimately, depended upon the subsequent inability of the other party to hold it, e.g., promotion, sickness or death. Consequently, such traffic often gave rise to the hope, or in some instances, the attempt, of removing the person whose presence impeded the return of the benefice. Again, such transfers of benefices upon private authority were analogous to hereditary succession, which has always been contrary to the mind of the Church.

The notions of confidential simony have been preserved in the Code,[89] where the Ordinary is forbidden to allow the resignation of a benefice in favor of another, or with any condition pertaining to the disposal of the benefice itself or the fruits thereof. When a benefice becomes vacant by resignation or a sentence of privation, the superior who accepted the resignation or pronounced the sentence cannot validly confer the benefice on his own relations by blood or marriage to the second degree inclusive, nor on his familiars. He cannot confer it upon the relations or familiars of the person who resigned it.[90] Confidential simony, however, is no longer *simonia qualificata,* carrying with it its own special penalties. In the Code it has been assimilated to common simony of the ecclesiastical law, and as such is subject to the sanctions placed upon conventional and real simony.

---

[89] Cans. 1486, 157, 146.

[90] Can. 157 makes this provision for ecclesiastical offices, but in virtue of can. 146, it may be applied also to benefices.

CHAPTER III

THE SIMONIACAL CONTRACT

Canon 729.—Firmis poenis in simoniacos jure statutis, contractus ipse simoniacus et, si simonia committatur circa beneficia, officia, dignitates, subsequens provisio omni vi caret, licet simonia a tertia persona commissa fuerit, etiam inscio proviso, dummodo hoc non fiat in fraudem ejusdem provisi aut eo contradicente. Quare:

1.° Ante quamlibet judicis sententiam res simoniace data et accepta, si restitutionis sit capax nec obstet reverentia rei spirituali debita, restitui debet, et beneficium, officium, dignitas dimitti;

2.° Simoniace provisus non facit fructus suos; quod si eos bona fide perceperit, prudentiae judicis vel Ordinarii permittitur fructus perceptos ex toto vel ex parte eidem condonare.

Simony of its very nature usually implies complicity. Hence, after fully describing the nature of simony, the legislator turned his attention to the contract or agreement which existed between the parties. In both simony of the divine law and simony of the ecclesiastical law, the object of the contract is not salable. It follows as a natural consequence that any negotiations regarding such an object are invalid.[1] The Church lays down as one of the requisites for the acquisition of benefices, offices and dignities, that appointments be free from venality. Simony in such matters would render the subsequent provisions null and void, even if the appointee had been ignorant of the crime. The sanction of the present law does not apply to the papal election, which is valid in spite of the simoniacal agreements, nor to the case where simony had been committed by a third party for the sole purpose of rendering the appointee ineligible, nor to

[1] St. Thomas, *Summa Theologica*, 2, 2, q. 100, a. 6.

the case where the recipient of the office had protested against the transaction. In the former case, the law would favor the malice of perverse men, if it were to invalidate an appointment in which fraud was involved.[2] It must be remembered that the nullity of the appointment is not in the character of a punishment as some authors[3] hold, but is rather a safeguard against greater evils. This is apparent from the very nature of punishments and the fact that it affects those who are ignorant of the simony.[4]

Article I.—Offices, Benefices and Dignities

Although the text of canon 729 considers simony in benefices before turning its attention to the abuse in offices, it seems better to invert the order to assure a more strict adherence to the method adopted by the Code. The subject of ecclesiastical offices is considered in the Second Book, while benefices are reserved to the latter part of the Third.[5] Furthermore, practically everything which might be said concerning ecclesiastical offices, can be predicated of benefices,[6] but the reverse is not true. To avoid tedious repetition, the legislation on benefices will be deferred until after the consideration of simony in offices.

§ 1. *Ecclesiastical Offices*

The term *office* can be taken in a broad sense to mean any function, exercised for a spiritual end in conformity with canonical rules.[7] Such would be the office of sacristan, organist,

---

[2] Schmalzgrueber, *Jus Ecclesiasticum Universum*, lib. V, tit. III, n. 266; Lessius, *De Justitia et Jure*, c. 35, n. 143; Suarez, *Opera Omnia*, tom. XIII, lib. IV, c. 57, n. 33.

[3] De Meester, *Compendium*, III, n. 1111.

[4] "Sine culpa, nisi causa subsit, non est aliquis puniendus."—Reg. 23, R. J., in VI°. St. Alphonsus, *Theologia Moralis*, lib. III, n. 112, ad. 2; Pichler, *Jus Canonicum*, lib. V, tit. III, n. 60; St. Thomas, *Summa Theologica*, 2, 2, q. 100, art. 6, ad 6.

[5] In can. 2392, offices precede benefices.

[6] Can. 146.

[7] Can. 145, § 1; Wernz-Vidal, *Jus Canonicum*, II, n. 140; Chelodi, *Jus de Personis*, n. 131; Maroto, *Institutiones, Juris Canonici*, II, n. 578; Pruemmer, *Manuale Juris Canonici*, q. 72.

delegated judge, confessor, preacher. In this sense it implies, either no jurisdiction at all, as in the case of the sacristan or organist, or at most power which has been delegated.[8] It may signify a function which is exercised entirely in temporalities, which, however, are directed to a spiritual end, or it may deal entirely with spiritual duties.[9]

In its stricter sense, an ecclesiastical office is a function established by either divine or ecclesiastical authority, permanent in character, to be conferred in the form prescribed by the canons, and implying some participation in ecclesiastical power, either of Orders or of jurisdiction.[10] Thus the office of Sovereign Pontiff, the episcopate, the pastorate and the Superiorship of exempt clerical religious institutes would be offices in the strict sense of the term.[11]

There are five constituent elements in an ecclesiastical office:

1. *A spiritual function,* i.e., spiritual in its origin, its end or its object. The office should be constituted, not for the exercise of a function which is common to everyone who is ordained, such as the private recitation of the office or the private celebration of Mass, but should involve some special power, either of Order or of jurisdiction. Ordination does not confer an office, but rather the office is conferred upon the ordained. Hence the spiritual function should be distinct from what is the common obligation or privilege of ordination.[12]

2. *Divine or ecclesiastical institution.* The papacy and the episcopate are of divine origin[13] whereas the other offices, such as the archbishopric, metropolitan, etc., are of ecclesiastical origin.

3. *Perpetuity.* Where an office is instituted by lawful author-

---

[8] Chelodi, *loc. cit.*, n. 131.

[9] Wernz-Vidal, *loc. cit.*, n. 140, II.

[10] Can. 145, § 1.

[11] Vermeersch-Creusen, *Epitome,* I, n. 227, 1o; Blat, *Commentarium,* II, n. 85.

[12] Wernz-Vidal, *Jus Canonicum,* II, n. 140, 2o.

[13] Can. 108, § 3; Chelodi, *Jus De Personis,* n. 132; Cocchi, *Commentarium,* lib. II, n. 59, 2o; Wernz-Vidal, *Jus Canonicum,* II, n. 140, 1o; Pruemmer, *Manuale Juris Canonici,* q. 72; Maroto, *Institutiones,* II, n. 579.

ity, and a titular appointed to it, so that the office does not cease with him, but merely becomes vacant, this office is said to possess objective stability. In this sense, an office differs from a function instituted only for a period of time and dependent upon the will of the superior.[14] Objective stability is necessary for an ecclesiastical office, but it is not essential that the office be transferred to the successor without any interruption. It is sufficient that, when the same circumstances or exigencies arise, the office be conferred, e.g., the office of Vicar Capitular or Administrator.[15] Subjective perpetuity, which implies that the appointee is irremovable, is not essential to an ecclesiastical office.[16]

4. *Canonical provision.* Appointment to ecclesiastical offices should be made according to the prescriptions of the canons and by the legitimate superior. The rights and obligations connected with the office should be determined in its institution, and not in individual cases, as is true in delegation or in the functions whose rights and obligations are stipulated in a contract.[17]

5. *Ecclesiastical power of Order or jurisdiction.* The power thus annexed to the office is ordinary, and cannot be increased or diminished at will by the superior.[18] It may pertain to the internal forum alone, as in the office of pastor, to the external forum alone, as the office of Rotal official, or to both fora, as the bishopric.[19]

In law, the term *office* is to be taken in its strict sense, unless the context prescribes otherwise.[20] Hence where the Code simply mentions offices, the principle will not hold, *ubi lex non distinguit, neque nos distinguere debemus,* unless it is quite evident that the context includes office in the broad as well as the

---

[14] Wernz-Vidal, *loc. cit.;* Chelodi, *loc. cit.;* Pruemmer, *loc. cit.;* Maroto, *loc. cit.*, b.

[15] Vermeersch-Creusen, *Epitome*, I, n. 227; Wernz-Vidal, *loc. cit.*, III.

[16] Maroto, *loc. cit.*

[17] Wernz-Vidal, *loc. cit.*, II, 2o; Chelodi, *loc. cit.*, n. 131.

[18] Wernz-Vidal, *loc. cit.*, Chelodi, *loc. cit.*, Maroto, *loc. cit.*, n. 579, d.

[19] Maroto, *loc. cit.*, e, nota; Cocchi, *Commentarium,* lib. II, n. 59, 2o.

[20] Can. 145, § 2.

restricted sense.[21] In the present canon there seems to be no reason to justify the broad interpretation,[22] though some authors[23] insist that all offices are included.

It is not necessary to consider in detail the various kinds of offices, since the law is general. For the sake of clarity, it will be sufficient to make the three-fold division with Vermeersch.[24] Offices may be considered as beneficial or non-beneficial in so far as they have annexed to them the right of receiving the fruits accruing to them. They are major or minor, in so far as they confer episcopal or quasi-episcopal power or not. They are called religious or secular from the quality of the subjects who may be appointed to them.

Since simony is concerned usually with the acquisition of offices, it might be well to examine the various methods of canonical provision or appointment. Canonical provision consists in the granting of an office according to the norms established by law.[25] This involves the designation of the person, the granting of the title, and the installation or investiture.[26] Designation of the person may be made either at the free choice of the superior, (*libera collatio*); by presentation of the candidate by a patron; by election; by postulation, as in the case of a candidate who is bound by some impediment.[27] Concession of the title is made either by the superior who has the right of designation or appointment; by institution, that is, when the superior confers the office upon the one suggested by the patron; by admission, if the choice of the electors is a postulate. Intro-

---

[21] Vermeersch-Creusen, *Epitome,* I, n. 227, 2o.

[22] Those who favor the strict interpretation are: Cappello, *De Censuris,* n. 361, 2o; Cocchi, *Commentarium,* lib. V, n. 274, a; Chelodi, *Jus Poenale,* n. 104; Noldin, *De Censuris,* n. 84, b; Blat, *Commentarium,* lib. V, n. 237; Farrugia, *Commentarium in Censuras,* n. 144; Augustine, *A Commentary,* IV, 14.

[23] Cerato, *Censurae Vigentes,* n. 65; Sole, *De Delictis et Poenis,* n. 457; Pistocchi, *I Canoni Penali,* p. 332.

[24] Vermeersch-Creusen, *Epitome,* I, n. 228.

[25] Can. 147, § 2.

[26] Wernz-Vidal, *Jus Canonicum,* II, n. 182, II, Chelodi, *Jus de Personis,* n. 133; Vermeersch-Creusen, *Epitome,* I, n. 230.

[27] Can. 148. Cf. preceding note.

duction to possession is a complement of canonical provision. It is designated by various names, such as, corporal institution, investiture, enthroning. Benefices, major dignities, the cardinalate, require investiture. Where no confirmation is required, a simple election suffices, and the action is complete when the candidate accepts the office to which he has been elected, as in the case of the Superior General of a Religious Institute of pontifical right.[28]

Since the filling of a vacant office by free collation is dependent upon the will of the Superior, any contract involving simoniacal appointment thereto, which he might make, is *ipso jure* null and void. In this form of simony ordinarily the contract exists between the grantor and the recipient, without the intervention of patrons, electors, or postulators. The price may be paid by either the appointee or a third party, and even without the knowledge of the recipient, provided, of course, that this was not done in fraud. Any temporal advantage which would be given in exchange for the office would be sufficient to constitute a simoniacal pact.

With regard to the institution of a person presented by a patron, or the confirmation of an election, there is even a wider field for illicit transactions. Stipulations can be made between the candidate and the patron or electoral body, between the candidate and the superior, or even between the superior and the patron or electors.

Pruemmer contends that if a person has secured the right, whether *ad rem* or *in re,* it would not be simoniacal for him to pay for the removal of any opposition to his confirmation or possession.[29] He argues that in this case, the person is not buying the office, but is simply removing unjust vexation. It is necessary, of course, that the opposition be unjust and the right certain. Thus, where the election has been without fault and the candidate is worthy, refusal of confirmation must be considered illegal and unjust opposition.[30] This view is not only rejected by many post-Code writers, but also seems to be in

---

[28] Can. 148; Vermeersch-Creusen, *Epitome,* I, n. 231, 4o.

[29] *Manuale Theologiae Moralis,* II, n. 563, 6o.

[30] Can. 177, § 2.

conflict with the opinion which was quite general under the old legislation. In the present case, authors distinguish between the *jus ad rem,* that is, the right which one has that an object become his own, and the *jus in re,* or the right which he has to a thing already his own. The *jus ad rem* affects not the thing itself, but some person, whereas the *jus in re* touches the thing itself.[31] By election or presentation, one acquires the *jus ad rem,* which he can oblige his superior to recognize.[32] All admit, that once the *jus in re* has been acquired, the removal of opposition by the appointee would not be simoniacal, since he is paying for something which is material in itself.[33] It should be noted, however, that even where it is licit to pay for the removal of opposition, the object given in such payment must be strictly material. To give a spiritual object would be simony, since it would involve the transfer of a spiritual thing for something material, i.e., the removal of the unjust opposition.[34] When, however, the right which is acquired, is merely the *jus ad rem,* as in the case of election, authors are agreed that it is simoniacal to secure the *jus in re* by the payment of a price for the removal of the opposition. By this payment is secured not only something temporal, that is, the cessation of unjust vexation, but also the spiritual right. The opposition will not be removed except by the contrary action, the confirmation or the admission. Hence when one pays a superior to remove his opposition he really pays him to place the opposite act, or confirm his election.[35] If, however, after confirmation or admission, one's physi-

---

[31] Noldin, *Summa Theologiae Moralis,* I, n. 270.

[32] Vermeersch-Creusen, *Epitome,* I, n. 231, 3o; Chelodi, *Jus de Personis,* n. 133; Maroto, *Institutiones,* II, n. 586, B.

[33] Navarrus, *Manuale,* c. 23, n. 102; Laymann, *Theologia Moralis,* lib. IV, c. 50, n. 2; Lessius, *De Justitia et Jure,* lib. II, c. 35, n. 110; Reiffenstuel, *Jus Canonicum Universum,* lib. V, tit. III, n. 309; Schmalzgrueber, *Jus Ecclesiasticum Universum,* lib. V, tit. III, n. 134; St. Alphonsus, *Theologia Moralis,* lib. III, c. 2, n. 99; Noldin, *Summa Theologiae Moralis,* II, n. 196; Genicot, *Institutiones Theologiae Moralis,* I, n. 288, V, 3o; De Meester, *Compendium,* III, n. 1109; Ferreres, *Compendium Theologiae Morālis,* I, 378.

[34] Schmalzgrueber, *loc. cit.,* n. 140, 3o.

[35] Schmalzgrueber, *loc. cit.,* n. 136; Alphonsus, *loc. cit.,* n. 100.

cal possession of the office were impeded, payment for the removal of such opposition would not involve simony, since possession is something purely temporal.[36]

§ 2. *Benefices*

A benefice is a juridical entity, established or erected in perpetuity by competent ecclesiastical authority, consisting of a sacred office and the right to receive the revenue accruing thereto.[37] It is a juridic entity or non-collegiate moral person whose existence is independent of the person who instituted it and the one who possesses it.[38] The Code has settled definitely the conflict of opinions regarding the stability necessary for the constitution of a benefice. Many, under the old legislation,[39] required both subjective and objective perpetuity, at least as far as benefices in the strict sense were concerned. The present law stresses objective stability by placing special emphasis upon the *juridical entity*.

For the erection of benefices inferior to the episcopacy, and not reserved to the Holy See, the authority of the Bishop is sufficient. This is evident not only from canon 1414, § 2, but also from the constant discipline of the Church.[40] The sacred office to which is attached the right of revenues was examined above. The word *right* is used advisedly, because the beneficiary retains this right even though the property may have been taken away, e.g., by the State, and as a result he receives no revenue.

The Code is quite explicit regarding the endowment of a

---

[36] Schmalzgrueber, *loc. cit.*, n. 142; Suarez, *Opera Omnia*, tom. XIII, lib. IV, tr. 10, c. 50, n. 32; Lessius, *De Justitia et Jure*, lib. II, c. 35, n. 110; Laymann, *Theologia Moralis*, lib. IV, tr. 10, c. 8, n. 22; St. Thomas, *Summa Theologica*, 2, 2, q. 100, art. 2, ad. 5.

[37] Can. 1409.

[38] Cocchi, *Commentarium*, lib. III, pars. V, n. 81; Pruemmer, *Manuale Juris Canonici*, q. 442.

[39] Lessius, *De Justitia et Jure*, lib. II, c. 34, n. 3; Pirhing, *Jus Canonicum*, lib. III, tit. V, n. 3; Schmalzgrueber, *Jus Ecclesiasticum Universum*, lib. III, tit. V, n. 4; Reiffenstuel, *Jus Canonicum Universum*, lib. III, tit. V, n. 52; Pennacchi, *Commentaria in Const. "Apostolicae Sedis,"* I, 831.

[40] Schmalzgrueber, *loc. cit.*, n. 6; Pennacchi, *loc. cit.*, p. 832.

benefice. This endowment may consist either of property belonging to the benefice, tithes, voluntary though secure offerings of the people, stole fees, or choral distributions.[41] The first two elements mentioned in the constitution of a dowry are by no means new. The third, however, is an innovation. It was agreed, before the Code, that taxes imposed on the faithful might constitute the revenue, but not voluntary offerings.[42] Opinion was divided concerning the constitution of beneficial revenue by stole fees. Under the new legislation, both of these may constitute the dowry, provided they are so determined by the Bishop. Choral distributions are unknown in the United States, since there are no cathedral or collegiate chapters. Such distributions consist in portions of the beneficial revenues given to the members of these chapters, who are actually present for divine office, or who are considered present by fiction of law.[43]

The presence and position of the word "quibuslibet" in canon 2392, where cognizance is taken of canon 729, makes it quite clear that all species of benefices are to be included in the sanction. Under the old law, benefices were taken in the strict sense,[44] and there is nothing in the present legislation which seems to call for a wider interpretation.[45] Hence, since the law includes all species of benefices in the strict sense, it will be unnecessary to delay upon a consideration of them here. It should be sufficient to mention in passing, those offices which, although bearing a resemblance to canonical benefices, are not considered benefices in law. Lay chaplaincies, or obligations of saying mass or performing certain duties in a chapter at stated

---

[41] Can. 1410. In reference to stole fees Ferry, (*Stole Fees*, p. 61), says: "That they can be employed for this end must now be admitted, but there is required the positive declaration of the Ordinary to that effect in erecting the benefice; since the enumeration of possible sources or revenue in canon 1410 is disjunctive, and not conjunctive, stole fees can be assimilated to the beneficial dowry only when truly ecclesiastical property is unavailable or insufficient to constitute it." Cf. Vermeersch-Creusen, *Epitome*, II, n. 798.

[42] Wernz, *Jus Decretalium*, III, n. 180.

[43] Can. 420.

[44] Pennacchi, *Commentarium in Const. "Apostolicae Sedis,"* I, 831.

[45] Can. 6, 3°.

hours, but established without the intervention of ecclesiastical authority; coadjutorships; personal pensions which, although they give the cleric a right to revenue, are not constituted in perpetuity; temporary commenda or grants of income from property on condition that, if the holder lose his claim, the revenue will revert to the Church; all these are not considered benefices in the strict sense of the word.[46]

§ 3. *Parishes in the United States*

A matter of more immediate interest is the canonical status of parishes in the United States, for if they are not benefices in the strict sense, the penalties for traffic in benefices cannot be applied to abuses in their acquisition or dismissal. While it must be conceded that, even if our parishes were not benefices, they are certainly ecclesiastical offices and hence come within the scope of this canon, nevertheless the provisions of the law peculiar to benefices cannot be applied unless it can be established that the American parish contains all the essentials of a canonical benefice. The history of parishes in our country is interesting and it might not be amiss to give in briefest outline its general features. In 1908, the United States, up to that time under the jurisdiction of the Congregation of the Propaganda, came directly under the common law of the Church. In the earlier days, scarcity of priests, fluctuating population and a general lack of organization resulted in priests being sent out with a sort of general care of the people in a more or less indefinite territory.[47] At the time of the First Plenary Council of Baltimore, benefices were known in possibly one place, New Orleans.[48] The Second Plenary Council made some progress by legislating that one pastor should be placed in charge of each territory, and, if necessary, assistants should be appointed to assist him in the care of souls.[49] The Council also prescribed

[46] Cans. 1412, 1413.

[47] Golden, *Parochial Benefices*, p. 98.

[48] Shea, *History of the Catholic Church in the United States* (New York, 1892), III, 414.

[49] 1866, *Acta et Decreta*, n. 111.

the division of the country into districts,[50] but unfortunately the law could not be observed in all localities. The Third Plenary Council provided that throughout the dioceses, certain missions should be selected to which irremovable rectors should be appointed.[51]

With the publication of the decree *"Maxima Cura,"*[52] parishes whose pastors were removable *ad nutum* were abolished. A doubt arose whether the prescriptions of the *"Maxima Cura"* applied to the United States. Canon 30 of the decree had expressly stated that it applied to all who held a parish under any title, whether they were called perpetual Vicars, *desservants,* or any other name. The Sacred Congregation of the Consistory stated definitely that the *"Maxima Cura"* applied to the United States.[53] However, the answer of the Sacred Congregation was not as general as might appear at first sight. The *"Maxima Cura"* did not change the character of those parishes and missions which were established by the Third Plenary Council of Baltimore, but whose rectors were removable *ad nutum Episcopi.* Removable rectorships in the United States remained *in statu quo* even after the decree.[54] Irremovable rectorships were to follow the prescriptions of the decree *"Maxima Cura."* From this it seems that there was some foundation for the opinion that irremovable parishes in the United States were really canonical parishes.[55]

The Code prescribes that the territory of each diocese should be divided into distinct territorial parts, each with its particular church and definite people.[56] Since the new law does not

---

[50] *Loc. cit.,* n. 124.

[51] 1884, *Acta et Decreta,* tit. II, c. V, n. 33. The Council did not intend that the rectors be canonical pastors, but merely hoped to approach this discipline as closely as circumstances would allow. It was the intention of Rome that canonical parishes should be erected by this council, but the Holy See decided to tolerate the conditions after hearing the Ordinaries. Cf. Golden, *Parochial Benefices,* p. 99.

[52] S. C. Consist., decr. *"Maxima Cura,"* 20 aug. 1910—*Fontes,* n. 2074.

[53] S.C. Consist., decl., 13 mar. 1911—*Fontes,* 2090.

[54] S.C. Consist., *"Statum Foederatorum Americae Septentrionalis,"* 28 jun. 1916—*Fontes,* n. 2090.

[55] Golden, *Parochial Benefices,* p. 100.

[56] Can. 216.

distinguish between irremovable and removable rectorships, when speaking of the establishment of parishes, it would seem only logical to conclude that such territorial divisions are really canonical parishes. Golden cites at least one diocese in the United States which has declared its parishes canonical.[57] An additional argument may be adduced from a response of the Sacred Congregation of the Consistory.[58] Treating of those dioceses which had come under the common law from the jurisdiction of the Sacred Congregation of the Propaganda, it rendered this conclusion. From canon 216 of the Code, it is evident that parts of the aforesaid dioceses, over which a particular rector has been placed for the care of souls, should in the future be considered parishes and ought to be called by that name. Hence, the parishes in the United States apparently must be called canonical parishes. Furthermore, our parishes can no longer be considered in that state of uncertainty which prompted the bishops in earlier times to request the Holy See to allow their missionary status. In its second paragraph, the response treats of the decree of erection, which might give rise to some doubt. Golden[59] argues, and it would seem rightly, that the decree of erection is required only in the establishment of new parishes, for, otherwise, there would be a manifest contradiction between the second paragraph and what has preceded. The Sacred Congregation definitely stated that the divisions of a diocese must be considered canonical parishes, without mentioning the decree of erection. It is presumed that the decree of erection is sufficiently given by the bishop's having defined the limits of the parish.

The two ideas of canonicity and benefice are almost inseparable, hence it was necessary to establish the canonical status of the parish before taking up the consideration of its claim to the title of benefice. According to the Code, three things are necessary for the constitution of a benefice; the sacred office, the right to the revenue, and the erection by ecclesiastical

---

[57] Boston, Sixth Synod, 7 April, 1919, nn. 21, 60.—Golden, *Parochial Benefices*, p. 101.

[58] 1 Aug., 1919—*AAS*, XI (1919), 346.

[59] *Parochial Benefices*, p. 103.

authority.[60] The first and third conditions are verified in the American parish, but there may be some doubt concerning the right to the revenue. The Code speaks of revenue as voluntary offerings of the faithful, which would be in the form of pew rents, block collections, yearly dues, Christmas and Easter collections.[61] Pastors in the United States usually receive a salary and, since the living expenses are taken from parish revenues, this salary is considered the amount necessary for his support over and above the rectory expenditures. Whatever he saves from his salary is his own property and consequently he may dispose of it as he sees fit; but any money saved in household expenses belongs to the parish. In some localities, the salary includes his household needs, and hence, whatever he saves from the expenses of the parish belongs to him. As has been said above, a decree of the Ordinary is necessary to constitute stole fees a means of beneficial revenue. It is very doubtful whether there are any dioceses in this country where all the money which comes into the parish is at the disposal of the pastor.

Golden[62] argues from the canonicity of our parishes that they must be considered benefices. "If we decide," he says, "that the parishes are canonical and refuse to admit that they are likewise benefices, where shall we find laws governing this sort of entity? Canon 1415 appears to make an exception for parishes that have not sufficient revenue, but where will we find any regulation for parishes which are canonical, have sufficient revenue, and still are not benefices? . . . When we look for the division, union, erection and the like, of parishes, we find it under the title of benefices." Augustine[63] raises a doubt about the national parishes in the United States, on the score that they are actually, and almost necessarily, more or less subsidiary and fluctuating. It is not exactly correct to say that they are only subsidiary, because their standing as independent entities is recognized by the Code.[64] While the law forbids

---

[60] Can. 1409.

[61] Golden, *Parochial Benefices*, p. 104.

[62] *Parochial Benefices*, p. 105.

[63] *A Commentary*, IV, 495.

[64] Can. 216, § 4.

the erection of such parishes without Apostolic indult, nevertheless it permits the existing national parishes to keep their identity and therefore their independence. To say that they are actually fluctuating seems to be somewhat inaccurate. National parishes, at least in the eastern districts of the United States, seem to possess as much stability as any other form of parish. As a rule, the people for whom the parish was erected, form a colony where they remain until external forces cause them to migrate elsewhere. They become attached to the church where their own tongue is spoken, where the clergy understand their customs, and they hesitate to change their residence because of the difficulty of finding such conditions in another locality. On the other hand, the members of parishes where English is spoken, have not such attachments. Almost every English-speaking parish is home to them, and it has been within the writer's experience to note that where English-speaking parishes have declined, national parishes, if anything, have increased and expanded.

To substantiate the opinion which ascribes a beneficial character to our parishes, the following letter, sent to the bishops of the country by the Apostolic Delegate, in November, 1922, is worthy of note.

RT. REV. AND DEAR BISHOP,

Notwithstanding the fact that several years have elapsed since the promulgation of the new Code of Canon Law, there still seems to be some uncertainty in the United States as to the nature of the parishes in this country and as to the consequent obligation of the pastors who are in charge of them. Both these questions have been debated in published articles from time to time. In order definitely to end this uncertainty I deem it my duty to communicate to you an official answer which I received from the Pontifical Commission for the Authentic Interpretation of the Canons of the Code.

Under date of March 20, 1921, I submitted to the said Commission the following *Dubium:*

"For the erection of a parish which has not the character of a benefice: (1ª pars.) is it necessary that the Ordinary should issue a formal decree declaring explicitly that he erects a certain district into a parish; or (2ª pars.) is it sufficient that, having divided a certain territory into several districts, the respective limits of which are definitely indicated, he assigns to each district a rector to take charge of the people and the church thereto pertaining, according to Canon 216, No. 1, and No. 3?"

Under date of September 26, 1921, His Eminence Cardinal Gasparri, President of the above-mentioned Commission, answered: "*Negative ad primam partem*," i.e., that a special decree of the Ordinary is *not* necessary for the erection of a parish; and "*affirmative ad secundam partem*," i.e., that it is sufficient, *Quoad Hoc*, for the erection of a parish, that the Ordinary define the territorial limits and assign a rector to the people and the church within said limits.

His Eminence, the President of the Commission, added, moreover, that *a parish is always an ecclesiastical benefice*,[65] according to Canon 1411, No. 5, whether it has the proper endowment (resources or revenue), as described and defined in Canon 1410, or even if, lacking such endowment (resources or revenue), it be erected according to the provisions of Canon 1415, No. 3.[66]

In the second *Dubium*, I asked further, if, after the promulgation of the New Code, a special decree on the part of the Ordinary was necessary to constitute as canonical parishes those which previous to the promulgation of the New Code had been established in the manner described in the second part of the first *Dubium*, as set forth above. The answer was that *no decree* is necessary, and that such parishes became canonical parishes, *ipso facto*, on the promulgation of the Code.

It is evident from this official answer, that all the parishes in the United States having the three necessary qualifications, viz. (1) a resident pastor; (2) endowment (resources or revenue) according to the provisions of Canon 1410 or 1415, No. 3; and (3) boundaries, are not only parishes in the strictly canonical sense, but are also ecclesiastical benefices. Hence pastors in the United States are real, canonical pastors, (parochi), having all the duties and obligations pertaining to such an office and (according to Canons 466 and 399) are specifically bound to apply the *Missa pro Populo* on Sundays and feast-days of obligation (including those that have been suppressed), this obligation binding them in conscience unless dispensation or commutation be received from the Holy See.[67]

Just how far the contents of the above letter affect other countries is open to question. Although the response is couched in general terms, it was given in answer to a query emanating from a particular country, and has never received promulgation in the *Acta Apostolicae Sedis*. Since the questions proposed by the Apostolic Delegate were in order to settle a doubt, the reply

[65] Italics inserted by the writer.

[66] "Non prohibetur tamen, ubi congrua dos constitui nequeat, paroecias aut quasi-paroecias erigere, si prudenter praevideat ea quae necessaria sunt aliunde non defutura."—Can. 1415, § 3.

[67] *IER*, XXXI (1928), 305-306.

was not merely declaratory. Until it is promulgated, it would seem to apply only to the United States.[68]

An anonymous writer in the *American Ecclesiastical Review*[69] would extend the notions of benefices to include even assistant pastorates, on the ground that they, too, possess the constituent elements of a benefice. The sacred office and objective stability of a curateship, he says, cannot be denied. The revenue arises from the custom of American Bishops' assigning a salary to curates, by statute. The validity of this argument is undoubtedly open to question.

§ 4. *Ecclesiastical Dignities*

An ecclesiastical dignity is a benefice to which is attached some jurisdiction and at least some preeminence or honorary prerogative.[70] In the present law, however, with perhaps the exception of prelatures, dignities generally lack jurisdiction and consist only of honor or precedence.[71] However, whether the dignity has jurisdiction annexed to it or not, it comes under the sanction of this canon, since the law makes no distinction. It seems to be the opinion of authors generally, that the law does not apply to dignities and offices of religious orders, except those which are offices in the strict canonical sense.[72] Cippolini holds that dignities which embrace no benefice or no *munus* strictly so called, are not included, for example, those who are members of the papal household, or Monsignors.[73]

§ 5. *Simony in Offices, Benefices and Dignities*

In general, the paying or receiving money for appointment, election or resignation of an office, benefice or dignity constitutes

---

[68] J. Kinane, "Did Missions in Countries such as Scotland, England, and the United States automatically become Parishes after the Promulgation of the Code of Canon Law."—*IER*, XXXI (1928), 307.

[69] *AER*, LXXVII (1927), 78, 79.

[70] Cappello, *De Censuris*, n. 154; Cippolini, *De Censuris*, p. 162.

[71] Sole, *De Delictis et Poenis*, n. 457; Cocchi, *Commentarium*, lib. II, n. 297; Ferreres, *Institutiones Canonicae*, I, n. 685.

[72] *Cappello, loc. cit.*, n. 361; Cippolini, *loc. cit.*, p. 164.

[73] *Loc. cit.*

simony proscribed by the present canon. Furthermore, ecclesiastical benefices should be conferred without diminution,[74] that is, without any innovation on the occasion of appointment, on account of which the benefice becomes less desirable or the burden more heavy.[75] Consequently the law condemns as simoniacal all deductions made from the revenues, all compensations or payments in the act of preferment, which accrue to the appointer, or to the patron or to others.[76] In parochial benefices, the Ordinary can impose pensions in favor of a pastor or coadjutor who retires from office, which pension must not exceed one-third of the entire parish revenues, after all expenses and uncertain revenues have been deducted.[77] The Bishop can permit the resignation of a benefice with the reservation of a pension in favor of the retiring pastor, which will last during the lifetime of the pensionary. But such reservations must be made in the act of conferring the benefice, not afterwards, and must be stipulated in the appointment.[78] He could not, however, impose a tax for the support of the seminary without consulting the proper Roman Congregation.[79]

Under the law of the Council of Trent,[80] any payments made in the act of provision were condemned if they accrued to the person bestowing the benefice or to the patron, but not such payments which were applied to pious uses, such as the building of a church or the support of some holy place, provided, of course, these reservations were not the result of a formal

[74] Can. 1440.

[75] Wernz-Vidal, *Jus Canonicum,* II, n. 217; Cocchi, *Commentarium,* lib. III, n. 118.

[76] Can. 1441.

[77] Can. 1429, § 2. "Note that the expression 'parish revenues' is not synonymous with the 'pastor's revenues.' Hence in our country only the pew-rent, plate and house collections, sure subscriptions and perhaps interest from money loaned would have to be considered. From these revenues the current expenses for the pastor's salary and the upkeep of the church, etc., may be deducted."—Augustine, *A Commentary,* VI, 514, 515.

[78] Pont. Comm. ad C.C. Auth. Interpr., 20 maii, 1923, *AAS,* XVI (1923), 116.

[79] Pont. Comm. ad C.C. Auth. Interpr., 16 oct., 1919, ad 16, *AAS,* XI (1919), 477.

[80] Sess. XXIV, *de ref.,* c. 14.

agreement. There seems to be nothing in the present law to call for a stricter interpretation.[81] The prohibition of money payments on the occasion of the conferring of benefices does not extend to the *annatae*, or certain portions of the fruits which are ceded to the Holy See.[82] Wherever the custom of paying this tribute obtains, it should be observed. The law of the *annatae* has never been introduced into the United States.[83]

Exchange of benefices is defined as the mutual resignation made upon condition that each of the resigners will receive the benefice of the other.[84] Alexander III in the Council of Tours (1163)[85] severely forbade the exchange of benefices, but such a prohibition was understood to refer to arbitrary transfers made upon private authority.[86] Exchanges could be made with permission of ecclesiastical authority.[87] It should be noted that there is no simony of the divine law involved in such transactions, since the temporal price is lacking.[88] Under the Code, an exchange of benefices without the consent of the Ordinary is invalid and simoniacal.[89] There are two principal reasons for the existing legislation. 1. No one can secure an ecclesiastical office without canonical provision; hence there is need of the intervention of the proper authority. 2. Beneficiaries have not the right to dispose arbitrarily of their benefices, which would seem to be the case, if they were permitted to transfer them by private contract.[90] Such an agreement would be licit, if it were subjected to the will of the superior, or in effect was a resignation of the benefices into the hands of the bishop upon

[81] Cocchi, *Commentarium*, lib. III, pars V, n. 118, c; Golden, *Parochial Benefices*, p. 54.

[82] Can. 1482.

[83] Augustine, *A Commentary*, VI, 541.

[84] Cocchi, *Commentarium*, lib. III, pars V, n. 153.

[85] C. 1-8, X, *de praebendis*, III, 5.

[86] C. 5, 7, 8, X, *de rerum permutatione*, III, 19; Suarez, *Opera Omnia*, tom. XIII, lib. IV, c. 31, n. 4.

[87] C. 5, X, *de rerum permutatione*, III, 19.

[88] Cocchi, *Commentarium*, lib. III, pars V, n. 156, proem.

[89] Can. 1487; Cocchi, *loc. cit.*, n. 156, d; Pistocchi, *De Beneficiis*, p. 495; Wernz-Vidal, *Jus Canonicum*, II, n. 342.

[90] Wernz-Vidal, *loc. cit.*, n. 337.

the condition that the benefices be mutually conferred on the resigners.[91] The term "competent superior" is used advisedly, because the Vicar General is expressly excluded unless he has a special mandate, nor does the Vicar Capitular or Administrator share in this power, even though the diocese has been vacant for a year.[92] If the benefices are in different dioceses, the consent of both Ordinaries is required.[93] The resignation is conditional, since it is made expressly for the purpose of exchange, and hence it will not become effective if the other party can not or will not resign his benefice. In such a case the party who has already resigned can recover his benefice without the formality of new collation, since the benefice has never been really vacant.[94]

If the benefices are unequal, the law is even more definite. In such circumstances, no compensation for the inequality can be made by reserving a portion of the fruits, or by the payment of any money.[95] There are four ways in which benefices can be unequal. 1. One benefice may be more opulent in both spiritualities and temporalities, e.g., a benefice of 250 acres of land with the obligation of mass and the office, and another of 100 acres with the obligation of the office alone. 2. One may be larger in spirituals, while the other's opulence might consist in a greater portion of temporal goods; as in the above example, the obligation of mass and office might be attached to the benefice of 100 acres. 3. Benefices may be unequal in spiritual burdens but equal in temporalities, as two benefices of 100 acres each, one having the obligation of mass and office, while the other only that of the office. 4. They may be equal in spiritual obligations, but unequal in temporal assets, as two benefices, one of 250 acres and the other of 100 acres, both carrying the obligation of mass and office.

---

[91] Pennacchi, *Commentarium in Const. "Apostolicae Sedis,"* I, 853; Wernz-Vidal, *Jus Canonicum,* II, n. 341; Vermeersch-Creusen, *Epitome,* II, n. 811, III.

[92] Can. 1487, § 1.

[93] Wernz-Vidal, *Jus Canonicum,* II, n. 339.

[94] Wernz-Vidal, *loc. cit.,* n. 341.

[95] Can. 1488, § 1.

In order to balance these offices, it is not permitted to deduct anything from the fruits, because, as has been stated above, benefices should be conferred without diminution. If the excess is in spirituals, compensation could hardly be excused from simony of the divine law, for the temporal price would be paid for something spiritual.[96] Where the inequality consists in the abundance of temporalities, such compensation, according to some authors[97] would constitute simony of the ecclesiastical law. It is true that such temporalities, when separated from the benefice, can be redeemed at a price, but such a separation is beyond the jurisdiction of the Ordinary. If the Bishop were to separate the fruits from the benefice, there would be an actual diminution in the conferring, which is forbidden. The Sovereign Pontiff may make such a separation, and permit the redemption of the temporalities.[98]

Article II.—Cooperation

If one knows that another will secure for him an office, benefice or dignity, through simony, and protests before the conferring, the transaction is valid, even though the other person in spite of his protest and without his knowledge, persists in the simony.[99] The expression "without his knowledge" is used advisedly, because if the appointee knows that simony has been committed by another, and nevertheless accepts the appointment, there seems to be nothing to excuse him from incurring guilt. By his acceptance, he consents to the fault and in effect becomes a cooperator in it.[100] The same would not be true if he had

[96] Can. 727, § 1.

[97] Cocchi, *Commentarium*, lib. III, pars V, n. 158; Vermeersch-Creusen, *Epitome*, II, n. 811; Suarez, *Opera Omnia*, lib. IV, tr. III, c. 34, n. 19; Navarrus, *Consilia*, lib. V, tit. III, cc. 25, 30, 50, 51; Pennacchi, *Commentarium in Const. "Apostolicae Sedis,"* I, 854.

[98] Vermeersch-Creusen, *Epitome*, II, n. 811; Wernz-Vidal, *Jus Canonicum*, II, 340.

[99] C. 33, X, *de simonia*, V, 3.

[100] Schmalzgrueber, *Jus Ecclesiasticum Universum*, lib. V, tit. III, n. 266; Suarez, *Opera Omnia*, tom. XIII, lib. IV, c. 57, n. 29; Lessius, *De Justitia et Jure*, lib. II, c. 35, n. 143; Pirhing, *Jus Canonicum*, lib. V, tit. III, n. 103.

merely a suspicion or fear that the crime had been committed.[101] Presumption that the person has consented to the simony can arise from the relationship of the one who made the payment. Thus if the simony had been committed by an enemy instead of a friend, the presumption would be in favor of fraud.[102] The refunding of the money paid by a third party might also give rise to the presumption that the beneficiary's opposition had been removed.[103] If the money were returned *before* the conferring of the office, it would be evident that the appointee had ceased to protest and had given his consent to the simony. Under such circumstances, the collation would be null and void. If, on the contrary, the payment were not made until after the collation, a distinction must be made. If it were evident that the money did not constitute an approbation of the other's fault, but rather a liberal donation in order that the other person might not suffer injury, there would be no simony.[104] On the other hand, if the money which was refunded after the conferring of the office, really constituted an approval of the simoniacal act, some[105] say that there would be simony involved, but that the conferring of the office would be valid. In such a case, it is presumed that the appointee's opposition continued up to the point when the price was refunded, and that he was ignorant of the simony at the time when he received the office. Hence when the office was conferred, all conditions for validity were fulfilled, namely protest and ignorance. The fact that at some time afterward he consented to the act, does not militate against the validity of a collation which has met the requirements of the law.[106] For example, John hears that James, a relative, intends to give the Bishop $100 in order that John may receive a certain parish. John protests against such action

[101] Suarez, *loc. cit.*, n. 30; Pichler, *Jus Canonicum,* lib. V, tit. III, n. 60.

[102] C. 33, X, *de simonia,* V, 3.

[103] C. 33, X, *de simonia,* V, 3.

[104] Navarrus, *Consilia,* lib. V, c. 16; Suarez, *Opera Omnia,* tom. XIII, lib. IV, c. 57, n. 31; Schmalzgrueber, *Jus Ecclesiasticum Universum,* lib. V, tit. III, n. 266; Lessius, *De Justitia et Jure,* c. 35, n. 144.

[105] Suarez, *loc. cit.;* Schmalzgrueber, *loc. cit.*

[106] "Quod semel placuit, amplius displicere non potest."—Reg. 21, R. J., in VIo.

declaring that he would not accept the parish under those conditions. James assures him that he will desist from his intention of giving the money, and will merely manifest John's merits to the Bishop. John receives the parish, entirely oblivious to the fact that the Bishop had been bribed. The parish had been conferred as the result of the simony of a third party, in spite of the beneficiary's protest, and without his knowledge. All conditions required by law are fulfilled, and the title to the parish is valid. Later, John hears that James had actually paid for the parish, and not wishing to give it up, he approves of the simony, and refunds James' money. It would seem that this subsequent action does not affect the title to the benefice. To say that the validity of an appointment would be suspended until the verification of a future act which might never occur, is to court absurdity. This, however, in no way limits the power of the competent superior to deprive such a one of his benefice in punishment for the crime. The present canon contents itself with declaring the juridic effects of the action itself.

ARTICLE III.—RESTITUTION

Since the title to things received and given is null and void from the beginning, restitution must be made even before the sentence of the judge. According to the natural law, restitution must be made before a sentence has been passed, only when there has been a violation of commutative justice, as for example, when the spiritual thing has no temporal value, as a blessing, dispensation, consecration, or when the object for which the temporal price has been paid is already due *ex officio*. Thus a pastor would violate commutative justice by charging for the teaching of catechism and the administration of the sacraments.[107]

This obligation of restitution before the sentence arises from the ecclesiastical law, and hence is binding even when there has been no violation of commutative justice. It binds not only in the case of benefices, but also in other matters.[108] Before the

[107] Noldin, *Summa Theologiae Moralis*, II, n. 189.

[108] De Meester, *Compendium*, III, n. 1111, 1o.

Code, the opinion was quite common that the spiritual object which was secured simoniacally should not be restored before a sentence had been passed.[109] Authors argued that spiritual things were of such a nature that either they could not be restored at all, or because of the silence of the law on the matter, a sentence of the judge was required to enforce the obligation. Under the existing legislation, this opinion is untenable, since the law expressly states that both what has been given and what has been received must be returned, without distinguishing the material from the spiritual.[110]

Two exceptions are made with regard to the restitution of objects secured through simony. There is no obligation if restitution is impossible,[111] or if the dignity of the spiritual object forbid it. Since the sacraments are valid if the essentials are observed,[112] it is evident that they cannot be restored. The same is true of acts of jurisdiction, such as dispensations, absolutions.[113] The reverence due the sacred thing would forbid its restitution in the case of the purchase of a relic from an infidel.

The temporal price must be restored even if the restitution of the spiritual object can not or should not be made, because the contract is null and void and the possessor has no right to the money received.[114] Since the Code does not specifically state *to whom restitution must be made*, the provisions of former laws, the opinion of authors as well as the general principles

---

[109] Pichler, *Jus Canonicum*, lib. V, tit. III, n. 63; Wernz, *Jus Decretalium*, VI, n. 348; St. Alphonsus, *Theologia Moralis*, lib. III, n. 113; Pirhing, *Jus Canonicum*, lib. V, tit. III, n. 185; Laymann, *Theologia Moralis*, tom. I, lib. IV, tr. 10, c. 8, n. 86; Suarez, *Opera Omnia*, tom. XIII, lib. IV, c. 59, n. 28; Schmalzgrueber, *Jus Ecclesiasticum Universum*, lib. V, tit. III, n. 284; Reiffenstuel, *Jus Canonicum Universum*, lib. V, tit. III, n. 286.

[110] Pruemmer, *Theologiae Moralis*, II, n. 565, 2o.

[111] "Nemo potest ad impossible obligari."—Reg. 6, R.J., in VIo.

[112] Leinz, *Die Simonie*, p. 78; De Meester, *Compendium*, III, n. 1111; Augustine, *A Commentary*, IV, 14.

[113] Augustine, *loc. cit.*

[114] De Meester, *Compendium*, III, n. 1111, 1o; Noldin, *Summa Theologiae Moralis*, II, n. 190; Reiffenstuel, *Jus Canonicum Universum*, lib. V, tit. III, n. 296.

of restitution must be considered.[115] The temporal price must be returned to the person who paid it.[116] This is especially true in the case where there has been a violation of commutative justice, for restitution must be made to the injured party, and the person who paid the price is the one who suffered injury. While it is true that one who has entered into such an unworthy contract deserves to be deprived of his property, nevertheless he is not directly despoiled by the law. Where there has been no violation of commutative justice, the question might be of different complexion. In this latter case, the obligation arises not from the natural law but from the ecclesiastical law. The question of restitution where commutative justice was not involved, was passed over in silence before the Code, principally because of the general opinion that such matters required the sentence of the judge. In penalty for a crime, the judge could order restitution to be made either to the church, to the poor or to some pious cause. But under the present law, the obligation of restitution is binding even before such a sentence. It would seem that the giver of the temporal price still retains his title to the money, and since the contract is vitiated, is entitled to his property. However, in view of the authority with which the opposite opinion is vested, and the lack of any definite pronouncement upon the subject, it must be conceded that where there has been no violation of commutative justice, restitution may be made either to the church, to the poor or some pious cause.[117]

Practically the same conclusion must be reached concerning the recipient of the spiritual object to be restored. Benefices which are conferred simoniacally, are reserved to the Holy See. The *jus patronatus* is extinguished.[118] Outside the case

---

[115] Can. 6, 3º.

[116] Pichler, *Jus Canonicum*, lib. V, tit. III, n. 65; Schmalzgrueber, *Jus Ecclesiasticum Universum*, lib. V, tit. III, n. 297; Sotus, *De Justitia et Jure*, lib. IX, q. 8, n. 1; Lessius, *De Justitia et Jure*, lib. II, c. 35, n. 170; De Meester, *Compendium*, III, n. 1111, 1º; Pruemmer, *Manuale Theologiae Moralis*, II, n. 565, 2º.

[117] St. Thomas, *Summa Theologica*, 2, 2, q. 100, art. 6, ad 3 et 5; Ferreres, *Compendium Theologiae Moralis*, I, n. 380.

[118] Can. 1435, § 1, 3°; 1470, § 1, 6°.

of benefices, however, the law makes no special provision for restitution to anyone except the owner. With regard to other spiritual objects, before the Code, it was held that the power of transfer on the part of the giver and the capacity of receiving in the person on whom the favor was conferred, were sufficient to constitute a legitimate transfer. Consequently, unless some impediment were present, the dominion of the spiritual object passed to the new possessor.[119] The mere fact that the spiritual object was given conditionally did not affect the title, since the condition, being unjust and malicious, was considered as not existing. Since they were convinced that the spiritual objects need not be returned at all, authors before the Code did not occupy themselves with the consideration of the person to whom they should be restored. However, in view of the positive precept, it would seem that things must be restored *in statu quo*, and the spiritual must be returned to its former owner.

Article IV.—The Fruits of the Benefice

If the spiritual object were a benefice, it must be dismissed at once. The terminology is precise, for the law does not mention resignation. Resignation would imply a valid title, which is absent in the case of simoniacal acquisition. Heretofore, attention has been called to the restitution of the spiritual object itself. Since the benefice has attached to it the right to the revenues or fruits, as they are called, provision has been made for their restitution. One who has been installed through simony, cannot lay claim to any of the revenue. This is merely a restatement of the natural law, for he cannot retain property to which he has no title, nor can he receive the fruits of property which is not his own.[120] Even though the invalidity of the title flows only from the dispositions of the ecclesiastical law, nevertheless, granting that the title is invalid, the obligation of resti-

[119] Schmalzgrueber, *Jus Ecclesiasticum Universum,* lib. V, tit. III, n. 284.

[120] Laymann, *Theologia Moralis,* tom. I, lib. IV, tr. 10, c. 8, n. 72; Pirhing, *Jus Canonicum,* lib. V, tit. III, n. 164; Suarez, *Opera Omnia,* tom. XIII, lib. IV, c. 57, n. 25; Schmalzgrueber, *Jus Ecclesiasticum Universum,* lib. V, tit. III, n. 267.

tution of the object and the fruits arises from the natural law itself.

In the matter of the restitution of fruits, a distinction must be made. If the one holding the benefice has committed simony himself, or if he has knowingly permitted another to do so in his behalf, he is a possessor *in mala fide.* Consequently, he must restore not only the object, and the fruits which are actually in existence, but also those which he has consumed in bad faith.[121] If, however, the simony has been committed by a third party, without the knowledge of the one who is installed, a further distinction must be made. As soon as the possessor in good faith discovers that the benefice does not belong to him and therefore he has not a legal title to it, he is bound to give it up. He must also return any fruits which are still in existence either *in se* or *in aequivalenti.* If he has consumed the fruits and has not thereby become richer, he is not bound to restore them or make any compensation.[122] In making restitution, however, a consideration for the bodily or physical exertion involved in the conferring of the benefice may be deducted from the amount to be restored.[123] This would be true even in the case of the possessor in bad faith; hence compensation for labor, e.g., in administration of the benefice, and manual stipends received while in possession may be retained.[124]

Article V.—Prescription

Before the Code, the opinion was quite general that, where simony was committed not by the possessor, and the good faith perdured for a period of three years, both the benefice and the fruits were given the favor of prescription, and neither had to

---

[121] Schmalzgrueber, *Jus Ecclesiasticum Universum,* lib. V, tit. III, n. 267; Tanquerey, *Synopsis Theologiae Moralis,* III, n. 508; Genicot, *Institutiones Theologiae Moralis,* I, n. 531; Pruemmer, *Manuale Theologiae Moralis,* II, n. 217.

[122] Tanquerey, *Synopsis Theologiae Moralis,* II, n. 499.

[123] Augustine, *A Commentary,* IV, 15.

[124] Tanquerey, *Synopsis Theologiae Moralis,* III, n. 509; Genicot, *Institutiones Theologiae Moralis,* I, n. 532.

be restored.[125] Authors held that the 36th rule of the Apostolic Chancery,[126] upon which the law of prescription was based, required interpretation. The term, *absque simoniaco ingressu*, was to be understood as applying to those who secured a benefice through a simoniacal act of their own, or who knowingly accepted a benefice which had been obtained through the simony of another. Under such circumstances, the possession was not in good faith, and the title was vitiated. In other words, the rule must be interpreted broadly in so far as it is favorable, and restricted in so far as it is unfavorable. Hence, if one had received a benefice in good faith, and held peaceful possession of it for a period of three years, he would secure not only the title to the benefice, but also the possession of the fruits. The text of the provision in the Code, however, seems to be more emphatic. No mention of the *ingressus* is made, but the Code merely states that the law of triennial prescription will hold *dummodo absit simonia.* Many authors after the Code content themselves with the mere transcription of the canon and make no note of the opinions which flourished under the old discipline. The codifiers knew of the opinion which enjoyed at least extrinsic probability, exempting the possessor in good faith from the rule of the Apostolic Chancery. If they wished to reject this opinion as improbable and contrary to the mind of the Church, why did they not make mention of this fact when casting canon 1446? On the other hand, where the law makes no distinction, neither should the commentator. In canon 729, the law defines just when simony is present in benefices. In canon 1446, it merely mentions that the law of prescription will not hold in the case of simony in benefices. It would seem that canon 1446 must be interpreted in the light of canon 729. Consequently even the possessor in good faith cannot enjoy the benefit of prescription.

---

[125] Schmalzgrueber, *Jus Ecclesiasticum Universum,* lib. V, tit. III, n. 267; Lessius, *De Justitia et Jure,* c. 35, n. 140; Garcia, *De Beneficiis,* p. VIII, c. 1, n. 15; Suarez, *Opera Omnia,* tom. XIII, lib. IV, c. 57, n. 39; Reiffenstuel, *Jus Canonicum Universum,* lib. V, tit. III, n. 278; Ballerini-Palmieri, *Opus Theologiae Moralis,* tom. II, tr. VI, n. 331.

[126] *Regulae Cancellariae Apostolicae,* XXXVI—Rigantius, *Commentarium in Regulas,* III, p. 156.

Article VI.—Condonation

The power of condoning fruits which have been received in good faith, is left to the prudent judgment of the Ordinary or ecclesiastical judge. If the crime is occult, application for condonation should be made to the Sacred Penitentiary.[127] The judge mentioned here is an ecclesiastical judge, even though the transgressor were a layman, for the Church reserves entirely to herself the right of judgment in such matters.[128] Thus, if the beneficiary in good faith were so poor that restitution of the existing fruits would plunge him into dire poverty, the judge or Ordinary could condone them. The faculties granted to Papal Nuncios, Internuncios and Apostolic Delegates are even more ample. Not only can they condone these fruits in the internal forum, but for a just and reasonable cause they can even convalidate the title to the benefice.[129] If a priest had secured his parochial benefice through simony, and there were insufficient priests to allow the dismissal of the benefice, the Delegate could convalidate the title. It is interesting to note that the faculties do not mention anything about the good or bad faith of the possessor. If the crime were occult, convalidation should be sought from the Sacred Penitentiary.

The provisions of the Code apparently refer to the condonation of those fruits which are still in existence either *in se* or *in aequivalenti*, for by the natural law one who has consumed in good faith is not bound to restitution, and condonation would be superfluous. Since the concessions of the *Index Facultatum* do not mention good or bad faith, it would seem that they extend to those fruits which have been consumed in bad faith, as well as those which are still in existence.

---

[127] Blat, *Commentarium*, III, n. 6.

[128] Can. 1553, § 1, 1o. Cf. Wernz, *Jus Decretalium*, VI, n. 349; Schmalzgrueber, *Jus Ecclesiasticum Universum*, lib. V, tit. III, n. 322; Wernz-Vidal, *Jus Canonicum*, VI, n. 26.

[129] *Index Facultatum*, apud Vermeersch-Creusen, *Epitome*, I, Appendix, I, n. 8; cf. Vermeersch, "Facultatum quae post Codicem Legatis Apostolicis concedi consueverunt Breve Commentarium," *Periodica*, XII (1923), 69.

CHAPTER IV

Offerings on the Occasion of Spiritual Ministrations

Canon 730.—Non habetur simonia, cum temporale datur non pro re spirituali sed ejus occasione ex justo titulo a sacris canonibus vel a legitima consuetudine recognito; item cum datur res temporalis pro re temporali, quae tanquam subjectum habeat adnexum aliquid spirituale, ex. gr., calix consecratus, dummodo pretium non augeatur propter adnexum rem spiritualem.

The present canon finds its principal application in the vindication of simony those voluntary offerings made by the faithful on the occasion of the administration of the sacraments. The theory of sacramental oblations is based upon Sacred Scripture itself. In the Gospel of St. Matthew[1] is found, "The workman is worthy of his meat"; and again in St. Luke,[2] "The laborer is worthy of his hire"; while St. Paul[3] writes: "Who serveth as a soldier, at any time at his own charges. . . . If we have sown unto you spiritual things, is it a great matter if we reap your carnal things? . . . Know you not that they who work in the holy place, eat the things that are of the holy place; and they that serve the altar, partake with the altar? So also the Lord ordained that they who preach the gospel, should live by the gospel." While these texts serve but to indicate the obligation of the faithful to support the clergy[4] and in no way authorize the making of oblations on the occasions of spiritual ministrations,[5] nevertheless, it seems only logical that those who receive special service at the hands of the ministers should contribute to their support by offerings at the time of these ministrations.

---

[1] Matt. X, 10.

[2] Luke, X, 7.

[3] I Cor., IX, 7, 11, 13, 14.

[4] Cornelius a Lapide, *Comment. in Sac. Script.* in I Cor., IX, 12, 14.

[5] Keller, *Mass Stipends,* p. 23; Ferry, *Stole Fees,* p. 12.

ARTICLE I.—SIMONY AND SACRAMENTAL OBLATIONS

A consideration of the theory and practice of sacramental oblations is of immediate interest in the present study, only in so far as it entails a defense of the Church against the charge of encouraging a practice which is simoniacal and therefore reprehensible. If such generosity of the faithful were tainted with simony, this simony would be of the divine law or of the ecclesiastical law. Sacramental oblations do not constitute simony of the divine law, for there is lacking perhaps the most important constituent element of simony—the will to buy and sell. The money offered on such solemn occasions is not given for the sacrament itself, or even for the labor expended in its administration, but for the support of the minister. The faithful have always realized that the sacraments were so precious that they could neither be bought nor sold, nor was there ever any misunderstanding that the oblation was the price of the priestly ministration.[6] Such colloquialisms as a "five dollar mass," or "baptismal fees," are traceable to the poverty of our idiom, rather than to any irreligious intention. The purity of intention on the part of the minister can be shown clearly from the fact that the ministration is in no way dependent upon the fee and cannot be refused for lack of it.[7] Such oblations cannot be branded as simony of the ecclesiastical law, because the Church, far from forbidding the practice, has reprobated the proposition which characterized them as an abuse.[8] It would be difficult to reconcile her vehement opposition to simoniacal practices with an open espousal of a theory which in itself is simoniacal. The mere fact that at times she has forbidden even the acceptance of voluntary offerings on the occasion of the administration of the sacraments,[9] and at a later date approved of them,[10] does not militate against the nature of these offerings. It is

---

[6] Gasquet, *Parish Life in Mediaeval England,* p. 187.

[7] Vogt, *Das kirchliche Vermögensrecht,* § 39, 1; Ferry, *Stole Fees,* p. 12.

[8] Pius VI, const. "*Auctorem fidei,*" 28 aug. 1794, prop. 54, Synodi Pistorien., damn.—*Fontes,* n. 475.

[9] Council of Elvira, (305), c. 48—Mansi, II, 13, 14.

[10] Council of Braga, (572), c. 7—Mansi, IX, 840.

merely an evidence of the ability of the Church to adapt laws framed in virtue of her own merely ecclesiastical authority to the needs of changing times and circumstances,[11] when stole fees were introduced by custom to take the place of personal tithes, which had fallen into desuetude.[12]

It is generally admitted that the obligation of making sacramental offerings arises from justice.[13] Hence, even clerics who have a sufficiency of this world's goods can receive or even demand the oblations which the law of the Church or custom decrees. When, however, a pastor or a beneficiary has the obligation of administering the sacraments, he cannot demand a stipend for such labor. Thus a pastor could not demand a stipend for preaching or administering the sacraments to his own flock,[14] or for the *missa pro populo*,[15] for his very office implies the obligation to perform these services for those under his care. Diocesan statute or legitimate custom can assign to the pastor certain fees, but under no circumstances can he make such charges upon his own authority.[16] Even where the statute or custom has provided for stole fees, the pastor cannot enforce his right,[17] nor can he refuse the sacraments to those who cannot pay the stipulated tax.[18] In speaking of stipends for ministrations which are due *ex officio*, authors[19] argue that the pastor has no right to a stipend, since his ministrations are really the fulfillment of an obligation of justice. Hence an injustice is done by such demands, and externally at least, simony is pre-

---

[11] Weber, *A History*, p. 11.

[12] Pichler, *Jus Canonicum*, lib. V, tit. III, n. 21, ad 1.

[13] C. ult., C. I, q. 2; Suarez, *Opera Omnia*, tom. XIII, lib. IV, c. 46, n. 7; Laymann, *Theologia Moralis*, lib. IV, tr. 10, c. 8, n. 14; Pirhing, *Jus Canonicum*, lib. V, tit. III, n. 128; Pichler, *Jus Canonicum*, lib. V, tit. III, n. 21; Reiffenstuel, *Jus Canonicum Universum*, lib. V, tit. III, n. 193; Schmalzgrueber, *Jus Ecclesiasticum Universum*, lib. V, tit. III, n. 94.

[14] Can. 464, 467, 468, § 1.

[15] Can. 466, 825, 2o.

[16] Can. 463, § 1.

[17] Ferry, *Stole Fees*, p. 49.

[18] Can. 463, § 4.

[19] Schmalzgrueber, *Jus Ecclesiasticum Universum*, lib. V, tit. III, n. 95; Ballerini-Palmieri, *Opus Theologiae Moralis*, II, tr. VI, n. 276, Pichler, *Jus Canonicum*, lib. V, tit. III, n. 19.

sumed. They generally add the parenthetical remark, "if he derives sufficient support from other sources." It would seem, in the light of this limitation, that if the pastor does not receive sufficient support from the congregation, he would not be acting unjustly to demand stipends for ministrations flowing from his office. The reason why one who is a beneficiary is obliged to perform certain spiritual functions freely, is because he is enjoying the fruits accruing to his office, and in return is bound to the service of the people. There would seem to be no obligation to such duties, unless the foundation of the obligation, namely sufficient support, were present. Custom and positive law play important rôles in justifying fees for ministrations which flow from an office, e.g., the universal practice of pastors' receiving fees for the administration of the sacraments.[20] However, "nowhere in the Code is it stated that parochial functions must have an offering or stole fee attached to them. Canon 1234 gives certain regulations to govern funeral offerings, and canon 1097, § 3, presupposes that offerings are made on the occasion of weddings, but with these exceptions there is no direct mention of stole fees in connection with parochial functions. The silence of the legislator on this point is an obvious indication that it is left to local custom to determine what functions shall have stole fees attached to them, and canonists who comment on this question are agreed that this is the case."[21]

§ 1. *Canonical Title*

The receiving of oblations is limited to circumstances justified and recognized by the canons or legitimate custom. Before the Code, canonists and moralists[22] justified the demanding of larger

[20] Noldin, *Summa Theologiae Moralis,* II, n. 194, b, c; S. C. C., *Lucana,* 17 dec. 1904—*ASS,* XXXVII (1904), 700.

[21] Ferry, *Stole Fees,* p. 41; cf. Vogt, *Das kirchliche Vermögensrecht,* § 39, 2.

[22] Schmalzgrueber, *Jus Ecclesiasticum Universum,* lib. V, tit. III, n. 98; Suarez, *Opera Omnia,* tom. XIII, lib. IV, c. 29, n. 15, 18; Lessius, *De Justitia et Jure,* lib. II, c. 35, n. 45; Bonacina, *De Simonia,* d. I, q. 6, p. 3, n. 2; Laymann, *Theologia Moralis,* lib. IV, tr. X, c. 8, n. 41, 42; Reiffenstuel, *Jus Canonicum Universum,* lib. V, tit. III, n. 305; Ballerini-Palmieri, *Opus Theologiae Moralis,* II, tr. VI, n. 278.

stipends or fees for the administration of the sacraments, when there was involved some grave inconvenience for the minister. This extrinsic labor or inconvenience had its value and could be remunerated, provided it were not due from justice. This same opinion has been adopted by many post-Code writers.[23] Looking squarely at the text of our canon, it would seem that it must be interpreted in the light of canon 736. Now canon 736 expressly forbids the minister to demand anything for the administration of the sacraments, under any pretext whatsoever, either directly or indirectly, except the oblations allowed in canon 1507. It is the right of the provincial Council to determine the taxes for the administration of the sacraments,[24] and local Ordinaries have no power to determine stole fees for their own dioceses.[25] Furthermore, the schedule of taxes adopted by the Provincial Council must be approved by the Holy See.[26] While it is true that the provincial Council may devise norms in consideration of extrinsic labor or inconvenience connected with the administration of the sacraments, it is hardly logical to say that in particular cases, the fixing of such fees is left to the individual.[27] The law makes no mention of extrinsic labor, except in the case of bination or trination. As often as a priest says several masses on one day, if one mass is applied for a stipend or from an obligation of justice, stipends cannot be accepted for the other masses. The law, however, allows some consideration to be made for the extrinsic labor connected with the other masses.[28] On Oct. 15, 1915, the Sacred Congregation of the Council had declared that the priest should not accept anything for the second and third mass on the Feast of

---

[23] Genicot, *Institutiones Theologiae Moralis*, I, n. 286; Pruemmer, *Manuale Theologiae Moralis*, II, n. 562.

[24] Can. 1507, § 1.

[25] S. C. C., *Dioecesis M. et Aliarum*, 11 dec. 1920—*AAS*, XIII (1921), 315.

[26] Can. 1507; cf. c. 250, § 2; 291, § 1; S. C. Consist., 21 apr., 1910—*AAS*, II (1910), 329, 330, where it is stated that the Sacred Congregation of the Council has competence in this matter.

[27] Cappello, *De Sacramentis*, I, n. 94.

[28] Can. 824, § 2. Exception is made, of course, for the feast of the Nativity, when a stipend may be accepted for each mass.

All Souls, not even for extrinsic labor.[29] Since this exception is omitted in canon 824, § 2, and in the light of the decision of the President of the Pontifical Commission for the Interpretation of the New Code, given Dec. 13, 1923,[30] this can be no longer held. Hence, while forbidden to accept a stipend for the second and third masses on the feast of All Souls, the priest can accept something under some extrinsic title.

It is not a question of simony of the divine law here, for it is presumed that the deliberate intention of accepting the stipend as a price for the spiritual, is not present. But in view of the very definite exclusion of every cause and every occasion for demanding anything beyond what is allowed by statute, it would seem that even compensation for extrinsic labor or inconvenience must be excluded also except where this is expressly permitted by law, and any violation of this provision would constitute simony of the ecclesiastical law.

§ 2. *Legitimate Custom*

Where the norm for fees to be given or demanded on the occasion of spiritual ministrations has not been established by the provincial council, recourse must be had to legitimate custom. The use of the term *consuetudo*, in preference to the expression *mos*, shows that the custom has the force of law.[31] Hence, the custom should be reasonable and enjoy legitimate prescription.[32] Custom can determine what functions demand offerings, the amount of these oblations as well as the recipient.[33] Thus, the practice obtains in many dioceses in the United States, of receiving donations from the people, and saying one mass for all on the feast of All Souls. Such a custom may be tolerated, provided the faithful are acquainted with the fact that only one mass will be offered.[34] Wherever laudable custom decrees that an

[29] *AAS*, VII (1915), 480, ad III.

[30] *AAS*, XVI (1923), 116.

[31] Keller, *Mass Stipends*, p. 92.

[32] Can. 27, 28; Cappello, *De Sacramentis*, I, n. 96.

[33] Can. 463, § 1; Ferry, *Stole Fees*, p. 38.

[34] S.C.C., 27 jan. 1877—*ASS*, X (1877), 120-126.

offering be made, the same may be received, asked and exacted without simony. Even threats of ecclesiastical punishment[35] may be used, for these penalties are inflicted rather for contumacy in refusing to abide by ecclesiastical statute and lawful custom.[36]

§ 3. *Excessive Demands*

If the minister should demand taxes in excess of the amount allowed by statute, doctors disagree whether he should be considered guilty of simony or not. It cannot be denied that he has a just title to the fee stipulated in the statute, but it is equally true that the excess is without title. The law expressly states that no simony is involved in the acceptance of fees on the occasion of spiritual ministrations, when such are recognized by the canons or legitimate custom, but excessive taxation is not only not sanctioned but is rather reprobated by the law.[37] Some authors[38] contend that such actions are not simoniacal because the minister has the right to some remuneration. An increase of taxes is nothing more than a violation of this right and hence a sin against justice rather than religion. While it is true that there is a right to some remuneration or emolument from spiritual ministrations, nevertheless this right is expressly limited in the law. It does not extend beyond the amount allowed by diocesan statute or legitimate custom. Anything over and above the stipulated sum, is without title, and since it is offered on the occasion of a spiritual function can hardly be excused from simony.[39] The protagonists of the opposite opinion contend that, provided there is no simoniacal intention, there

---

[35] Can. 2349.

[36] Ugolinus, *Tractatus de Simonia,* tab. I, c. 9, n. 7; Ferry, *Stole Fees,* p. 20.

[37] Can. 463, § 2; 736; 2408.

[38] Ferreres, *Compendium Theologiae Moralis,* I, n. 379; Vermeersch-Creusen, *Epitome,* II, n. 10; Fanfani, *De Jure Parochorum,* n. 240; Ferry, *Stole Fees,* p. 41.

[39] Cappello, *De Censuris,* n. 511, 3o, 1; Schmalzgrueber, *Jus Ecclesiasticum Universum,* lib. V, tit. III, n. 100; Gasparri, *De Eucharistia,* n. 557; De Meester, *Compendium,* III, n. 1106; Genicot, *Institutiones Theologiae Moralis,* I, n. 287; Reiffenstuel, *Jus Canonicum Universum,* n. 300.

is no simony involved. But the law judges only externals, and the circumstances certainly seem to indicate simoniacal intent, apart from the existence or non-existence of the internal feelings.[40] It is one thing to say that certain external actions are simoniacal, and quite another to prove that the internal affection corresponds to the external act.[41] The external violation of the law of taxes would seem to constitute at least a presumption of simony.

Vermeersch[42] declares without qualification that the acceptance of a stipend for a mass of bination is not a sin of injustice but of simony. He pursues the argument further, however, by declaring that, if a stipend has been accepted for the second mass, the recipient is not bound to restitution, since the donor received what his contract called for, and there was no violation of commutative justice. It is hard to see the foundation for this argument in view of canon 729, which expressly states that a simoniacal contract is null and void and restitution, if possible, must be made even before a sentence of the judge. Granting that such an action is simoniacal, the innominate contract is void and restitution is certainly possible without irreverence to the sacred thing. The mass cannot be restored but the stipend can and should be returned to the donor.[43]

§ 4. *Traffic in Mass Stipends*

Though the law expressly permits the acceptance of stipends on the occasion of the celebration of mass, the Church forbids all forms of commercialism in their collection and distribution.[44] The provision of the Code is little more than an echo from the Council of Trent,[45] which commanded bishops to safeguard the Holy Sacrifice from avaricious irreverence, exactions of alms,

---

[40] Can. 728, 2195.

[41] Cappello, *De Sacramentis,* I, n. 676; *De Censuris,* n. 511.

[42] Vermeersch-Creusen, *Epitome,* II, 10.

[43] One who demands more than is allowed by statute or custom does not forfeit the entire fee. Only the excess must be restored.

[44] Can. 827.

[45] Sess. XXII, *Decretum de Observandis, et Evitandis in Celebratione Missae.*

and everything else which might stain mass stipends with the taint of simony or venality. Even the appearance of negotiation or commercialism should be absent from mass stipends. Negotiation would consist in the collection of stipends and the retention of the surplus after engaging priests to celebrate the masses at a lower stipend. The appearance of negotiation would involve the collection of stipends with the intention of retaining part of them after securing the consent of the celebrant. *Mercatura* or commercialism implies the retention of the money received for the stipends, and in lieu of them, the giving of merchandise, such as books, magazine subscriptions, etc. This usually involves a commission on the stipends and a profit on the merchandise. If the merchandise were given instead of stipends but without profit, only the appearance of commercialism would be present. In practice, the distinction between traffic and the appearance of traffic is of little importance, since even the latter is forbidden by the Code. With reference to the keeping of part of the stipend with the consent of the celebrant, and the giving of merchandise in lieu of money, it would seem that the law condemns only those who collect stipends for this purpose. If the celebrant without compulsion foregoes the whole or part of a stipend, he is simply yielding his own right and this is no one's concern but his own.[46] He can accept merchandise instead of stipends as long as there is no appearance of commercialism in the transaction.[47] Where the merchandise is a magazine or periodical, it would seem that the acceptance of such goods is contrary to the mind of the Church. Keller[48] cites an unpublished response to the question whether publishers might lawfully send American magazines to European priests who could not afford to pay the subscription, but who would gladly say Masses for the intention of the publishers. The Holy See answered that such a procedure was not permitted.

While *mercimonium* and *negotiatio* require repeated actions,[49]

[46] Gasparri, *De Eucharistia,* I, n. 605; Keller, *Mass Stipends,* p. 140.

[47] Cappello, *De Sacramentis,* I, n. 680, f.

[48] *Mass Stipends,* p. 140. He does not mention the Congregation, nor the date of the response.

[49] Vermeersch-Creusen, *Epitome,* III, n. 524; cf. *Periodica,* I, (1905), 50.

the retention of a portion of a single stipend is forbidden unless the consent of the celebrant is freely given. In a founded mass, the excess of the diocesan stipend may be retained, provided the large stipend may be considered a partial endowment of the benefice or pious institution. In such a case it would be sufficient to send the manual stipend customary in the place where the mass is to be said.[50] Thus, if the endowment produced an income of $50, which was devoted to the support of the priest in charge of the chapel or shrine, it would be sufficient to send an amount equivalent to the manual stipend of the place where the mass is to be said. The amount of the manual stipend of the place where the founded mass originates, does not enter into the question. If the manual stipend in the place where the mass is to be said is $1, it would be sufficient to send $1, even though the diocesan statute of the place where the benefice or pious institution is located, demanded $5 for a manual mass. In manual masses, however, the celebrant is entitled to the entire stipend.[51] Two exceptions to this rule are mentioned in the Code. If the recipient is allowed by the donor to retain anything over and above the diocesan tax, or if he is certain that the excess were given for purely personal reasons, he may lawfully send an amount equivalent to his own diocesan stipend. Thus if a relative gave $25 for a low mass, the priest could be morally certain that the excess was given for personal reasons. Deductions may be made to cover the expenses of transmission, postage, etc.[52] An important distinction is made between the transmission of stipends for manual and founded masses. In the former case, where the conditions necessary for the licit retention of any excess are present, the amount of sender's diocesan tax must be forwarded. In the case of founded masses, the stipend of the diocese to which the stipend is sent, is of obligation.

Exchange of intentions does not seem to come within the scope of this prohibition, even though the stipends were un-

[50] Can. 840, § 2.
[51] Can. 824, § 1.
[52] Keller, *Mass Stipends*, p. 139.

equal.[53] Thus, Father John may say mass for the intention of Father James today, with the understanding that the latter will reciprocate on the following day. In such a case, the exchange is made willingly, and the matter of the stipends is the priests' own concern. Here, there would be neither simony of the divine law, since no buying or selling is involved, nor simony of the ecclesiastical law, because there is no prohibition against such a practice.

Article II.—The Union of the Material and the Spiritual

Canon 727 expressly declared that, where the relation is intrinsic, so that the material could not exist without the spiritual, the exchange of the spiritual for a temporal advantage would involve simony of the divine law. In the present canon, reference is made to an extrinsic union of the material with the spiritual. As has been noted above,[54] annexation of the spiritual and temporal may be antecedent, when the temporal thing existed prior to the annexation, concomitant when both originate at the same time, and consequent when the temporal follows or is derived from the spiritual. Concomitant annexation can be either extrinsic, when it is merely accidental and can be dissolved, or intrinsic if it is essential and indissoluble. Here the Code speaks of antecedent or concomitant extrinsic annexation, and the present canon was cast in view of the fact that such temporalities still retain their intrinsic value. The gold in the chalice has a negotiable value independent of its spiritual character. Thus, where the intrinsic value of the temporal object still remains, its sale would involve neither simony of the divine law, because it is a temporal object which is being sold, nor simony of the ecclesiastical law, for express permission is given in the law, provided of course, that the price is not increased on account of the spiritual character attached to the object. Therefore, it is licit to sell sacred vessels, vestments, consecrated graves, etc., provided no extra charge is made for their spiritual character. The sacred vessels should be melted or broken, the

[53] Cappello, *De Sacramentis,* I, n. 681.

[54] Chapter II, art. I, § 4, ii.

vestments torn or cut, or so treated that they lose their consecration or blessing.[55] It would seem that this limitation must be made only if they are to be devoted to secular use or sold to laics. There seems to be nothing to prevent their sale intact to another priest for sacred functions.[56] However, when such articles are sold to priests for sacred uses, they can be sold for their intrinsic value *qua talis*. Hence if there was $100 worth of gold in a chalice, the seller would not be obliged to accept only the amount corresponding to the value of the gold, but could demand its value as a chalice, together with expenses incurred in securing it.[57] When objects to which indulgences are attached are sold, even though there has been no increase of price, the indulgences are lost.[58]

---

[55] Schmalzgrueber, *Jus Ecclesiasticum Universum,* lib. V, tit. III, n. 163; Reiffenstuel, *Jus Canonicum Universum,* lib. V, tit. III, n. 225; De Meester, *Compendium,* III, n. 1098, 5o; Leinz, *Die Simonie,* p. 51.

[56] Schmalzgrueber, *loc. cit.*

[57] Schmalzgrueber, *loc. cit.;* Reiffenstuel, *loc. cit.*

[58] Can. 924, § 2.

CHAPTER V

Legal Sanctions

The necessity and justification of punitive sanctions flows from the very nature of law. Any legal system devoid of such sanctions would prove ineffectual in practice, defeating its own primary purpose of self-enforcement.[1] The Canon Law of the Church is no exception to this principle. Although the majority of the faithful are prompted to obedience by supernatural motives, nevertheless a stimulus in the form of additional penalties is necessary for those who respond not less promptly to threat and punishment than to the dictate of reason. The Church has discovered from sad experience that the sacred character of supernatural things was not sufficient to deter men from sacrilegious abuse of them. From the earliest times she has fortified her prohibitions with the most severe penalties, not only as a deterrent to crime but also to check the contumacy of men and to repair the scandal which had been given. Her censures for abuses of indulgences, the Sacraments, ecclesiastical offices, benefices and dignities have been preserved in the latest codification of her laws.

Before treating of the various sanctions placed upon the crime of simony by the Code, it might not be without profit to dwell for a moment upon a question which is passed over in silence by some authors[2] and settled quite dogmatically in the affirmative[3] or in the negative[4] by not a few. Before the Code, it was

---

[1] Ayrinhac, *Penal Legislation*, p. 21.

[2] Eichmann, *Das Strafrecht des Codex J.C.*, n. 80; Pruemmer, *Manuale Theologiae Moralis*, II, n. 566.

[3] Cerato, *Censurae Vigentes*, n. 65; Genicot, *Institutiones Theologiae Moralis*, II, n. 603; Pighi, *Censurae Sententiae Latae*, n. 94; Cippolini, *De Censuris*, p. 161; these authors contend that the censures apply only to simony of the divine law.

[4] Cappello, *De Censuris*, n. 360; Chelodi, *Jus Poenale*, n. 104, not. 4; Cavigioli, *De Censuris*, n. 148; Vermeersch-Creusen, *Epitome*, III, n. 597;

the common opinion among Canonists that the penalties laid down by the law were applicable only to simony of the divine law.[5] Controversy is still rife concerning the attitude of the Church at the present time. Arendt[6] argues that the notions of simony as set forth in canon 727, are in perfect accord with the teaching of the Doctors before the Code. Hence, according to the provision of canon 6, 2°, the present law must be interpreted in the light of preceding legislation, as well as in keeping with the jurisprudence of former times.

The discussion centers mainly upon the distinction between simony of the divine law and simony whose malice arises from ecclesiastical prohibition. The exchanges spoken of in paragraphs 1 and 2 of canon 727, says Arendt, are not to be understood in an univocal sense. Paragraph 2 bears only an analogical relation to the preceding one, the analogy being merely an analogy of proportion. Simony of the ecclesiastical law is not an intrinsic form of some other simony, but its relation is rather extrinsic, for by reason of a presumed danger of irreverence, such transactions are forbidden by the Church. Since, therefore, the danger of irreverence is the only reason why violations of the law come under the denomination of simony, their essential malice consists in a disregarding of authority, and not in any intrinsic evil. In the absence of any specific comparison of the spiritual and the temporal, as in paragraph 1, if it is true that the censures inflicted for simony of the divine law are also applicable to simony of the ecclesiastical law, then it must be admitted that irreverence which is less grave incurs most grievous penalties. This would seem to be a flagrant violation of the principles enunciated in canon 2218, 1°, which furnishes a norm for the interpretation of censures.[7]

Noldin, *De Censuris*, n. 84, a; these authors hold that the censures apply both to simony of the divine law and simony of the ecclesiastical law.

[5] Suarez, *Opera Omnia*, tom. XIII, lib. IV, c. 55, n. 5; Alphonsus, *Theologia Moralis*, lib. III, n. 108; d'Annibale, *In Const. "Apostolicae Sedis,"* n. 130. Exception was made, of course, of confidential simony, which, although of the ecclesiastical law, was a species of simony which had special penalties attached to it.

[6] "De Simoniae poenis l.s.," *Periodica*, XVIII (1929), 161 ss.

[7] Arendt, *loc. cit.*

While the point is well taken, it seems to prove little against the opposite opinion. Canon 727 expressly distinguishes simony of the divine law from simony of the ecclesiastical law, and gives clearly the genuine concept of both. No such distinction was made expressly in the old law, for paragraph 2 of canon 727 is new, as the lack of footnotes indicates. In the text on penalties, neither explicitly nor implicitly does the law make such a distinction. Hence the conclusion forces itself upon us, that where the law does not distinguish, no distinction is to be made. If the legislator wished to comprehend in canons 729 and 2392 only simony of the divine law, he should have expressed this in no uncertain terms. The objections raised by Arendt do not weaken this opinion. He argues that canon 2219 forbids expressly the extension of penalties from one case to another, even though the reasons for the application in the second case be more convincing. But the canon does not forbid extensions made by the law itself. And in the present case, the extension, if you will, has been made already in canon 727. When a term which requires interpretation is used in the code, naturally elucidation should be sought first from the Code itself.[8] Cerato contends that if the codifiers were solicitous enough to prefix the word *quibuslibet* to the expression *beneficiis, officiis, dignitatibus,* in order to show that the law embraced traffic in every kind of office, they should have made a similar clarification with the words *quaelibet simonia,* or *utriusque juris,* had they intended to sanction both kinds.[9] But such a distinction would have been superfluous in the Fifth Book, since it had been made already in the very definition of simony. By omitting any distinguishing notes, the legislator clearly shows that it was his intention to include every kind of simony which he has defined.

With some modifications, the censures for abuses of indulgences, the Sacraments, benefices, offices and dignities have been retained in the Code. The *ipso facto* penalties for simony in admission to the religious state and traffic in stipends have been suppressed.

---

[8] Can. 18.

[9] *Censurae Vigentes,* n. 65.

Article I.—Indulgences

Canon 2327.—Quaestum facientes ex indulgentiis plectuntur ipso facto excommunicatione Sedi Apostolicae simpliciter reservata.

Almsgiving has ever been recognized as a good work to which an indulgence might be attached. In this there is nothing essentially evil, for to give money to God or to the poor is a praiseworthy act, and if it is done from the proper motives, it will surely not go unrewarded. But no institution, however holy, has been entirely free from abuse. The avaricious saw in these pious practices an opportunity of raising money, and their action brought forth immediate condemnation from the Church.

Since one of the most common abuses consists in the deriving of material profit from the concession of indulgences, it might be well to consider those who are empowered by law to grant them. The spiritual treasury of the Church has been entrusted by Christ to His Vicar, and hence the Pope may grant indulgences to the whole world, without limitation as to kind, place or person.[10] The Pope, however, is not subject to the penal law of the Church.[11] The Code sets definite limits beyond which inferiors to the Sovereign Pontiff may not go in the granting of indulgences. Cardinals may grant an indulgence of two hundred days *toties quoties,* in any place or institution and to persons under their jurisdiction or protection. In other places they may grant the same indulgences but only to those present and for single times.[12] Archbishops have faculties to grant an indulgence of one hundred days in their provinces[13] while residential bishops may grant indulgences of fifty days in their dioceses.[14] They may also attach indulgences to rosaries, images or statues, but they must not exceed the limits of their jurisdiction. Apostolic Legates have faculties to grant six times a year, on the occasion of some solemnity, a plenary indulgence to all the

[10] Can. 912.

[11] Can. 1556.

[12] Can. 239, § 1, 34o.

[13] Can. 274, 4o.

[14] Can. 349, § 2, 2o.

faithful who under the usual conditions visit the church and pray for the intention of the Holy Father; a plenary indulgence to converts to the Catholic Church, at the time of their conversion; a plenary indulgence in particular cases on the occasion of missions; and an indulgence of a hundred days on two occasions to those who are present at their functions.[15] However, they should abstain from attaching indulgences to such devotional objects or acts of piety that have been thus enriched by the bishop within his territory.[16] Pastors and other priests who assist the dying are not only invested with faculty of bestowing the apostolic blessing with the plenary indulgence attached, but they are admonished not to omit the imparting of it.[17]

The penalty is incurred by those who derive material profit from indulgences, either by granting, publishing, applying or even by selling indulgenced objects at a greater price.[18] To incur the excommunication, it is necessary that at least part of the price be paid.[19] Thus, if the indulgence were granted and for some reason the money were not paid, the censure would not be incurred, for no material profit would be derived from the indulgence and the conditions required for the censure would not be fulfilled. Partial payment, however, would be sufficient to constitute simony. Some authors[20] hold that it is necessary that the price paid constitute grave matter in order that the transaction may come within the scope of this canon. However, it seems that, since simony of the divine law is involved, the external action is of sufficient gravity to warrant a canonical penalty, even though the price involved is only

---

[15] *Index Facultatum Legatorum Apostolicorum,* C. II, nn. 20-26—Vermeersch-Creusen, *Epitome,* I, Appendix.

[16] S.C. Indulg., 12 jan., 1878 ad IV—*ASS,* II (1878), 153.

[17] Can. 468, § 2.

[18] Cappello, *De Censuris,* n. 293; Chelodi, *Jus Poenale,* n. 67, 4o.

[19] Augustine, *A Commentary,* VIII, 317; Sole, *De Delictis et Poenis,* n. 351; Cappello, *loc. cit.;* Pistocchi, *I Canoni Penali,* p. 71; Cocchi, *Commentarium,* lib. V, n. 159, b; Cippolini, *De Censuris,* p. 132; Farrugia, *Commentarium in Censuris,* n. 81.

[20] Cerato, *Censurae Vigentes,* n. 54, 1o; Pistocchi, *I Canoni Penali,* pp. 71, 72.

slight.[21] Any contract in the matter is null and void and the price must be restored as far as possible.[22]

Before the promulgation of the Code, the penalty of excommunication inflicted for traffic in indulgences was incurred only by inferiors of Bishops.[23] These were punished by excommunication reserved in a special way to the Holy See. Bishops, Prelates and Cardinals, according to the provisions of Pius V, incurred interdict from entrance to the Church and privation of the fruits of their benefices until absolved by the Roman Pontiff.[24] This latter penalty was abrogated by the silence of Pius IX.[25] In the new law, all reference to the constitution *"Quam plenum"* has been omitted, and hence the present canon must be interpreted according to the preliminary canons dealing with the nature and scope of censures. Cardinals are exempt from the present sanction since they are not embraced by the penal legislation unless expressly mentioned. The privilege accorded Bishops is not quite so broad, for they immune only from *latae sententiae* suspension and interdict, where they are not expressly mentioned.[26] Since the present penalty is excommunication, Bishops are subject to the censure.

Former legislation included not only indulgences, but also other spiritual favors enumerated in the Constitution *"Quam plenum."*[27] Since the ratification of the censures connected with such abuses made special mention of the constitution of Pius V, it was concluded that only those abuses mentioned specifically by the Pontiff were subjected to the sanctions of the constitution *"Apostolicae Sedis."*[28] The present law contents itself with inflicting censure upon those who traffic in indulgences. Some authors[29] contend that the term *indulgence*

---

[21] Cappello, *De Censuris*, n. 293.

[22] Can. 729.

[23] S. Pius V, const. *"Quam plenum,"* 2 jan. 1570—*Fontes*, n. 132; Pius IX, const. *"Apostolicae Sedis,"* 12 oct. 1869—*Fontes*, n. 552.

[24] Const. *"Quam plenum,"* § 6.

[25] Pennacchi, *Commentarium in Const. "Apostolicae Sedis,"* I, 935.

[26] Can. 2227.

[27] Cf. Chapter I, art. V, § 3, ii, δ.

[28] Pennacchi, *Commentarium in Const. "Apostolicae Sedis,"* I, 936.

[29] Cerato, *Censurae Vigentes*, n. 54; Pighi, *Censurae*, n. 72.

embraces both true and false indulgences, since the law does not distinguish. However, both the constitution *"Quam plenum"* and the constitution *"Apostolicae Sedis,"* which essentially are the sources of the law of the Code, concerned themselves with true indulgences and hence there seems to be no reason to depart from the strict interpretation.[30]

Before the Code the law mentioned only those who derived material profit from indulgences as the subjects of the censure. The person who bought the indulgence or who paid the money was excused from the penalty since the law made no reference to accomplices.[31] Under the new legislation such an exemption cannot be made for traffic in indulgences by its very nature requires a cooperator, and such cooperators are considered equally guilty with the perpetrator of the crime, unless circumstances might excuse them from incurring the penalties.[32] Furthermore, it makes little difference whether the person selling the indulgence receives the money personally or through another.[33] Ignorance of the law or of the penalty, however, unless it were affected, crass or supine, would excuse from the censure, since the words *scienter, praesumpserit,* etc., are not used in the canon.[34] The fault cannot be excused on the plea of poverty or the promotion of some pious work.[35]

Article II.—The Sacraments

Canon 2371.—Omnes, etiam episcopali dignitate, aucti, qui per simoniam ad ordines scienter promoverint vel promoti fuerint aut alia Sacramenta ministraverint vel receperint, sunt suspecti de haeresi; clerici praeterea suspensionem incurrunt Sedi Apostolicae reservatam.

[30] Can. 6, 2o.

[31] Pennacchi, *Commentarium in Const. "Apostolicae Sedis,"* I, 938.

[32] Can. 2209, § 2.

[33] "Qui facit per alium, est perinde, ac si faciat per seipsum."—Reg. 72, R.J. in VIo. Cf. Sole, *De Delictis et Poenis,* n. 351; Pistocchi, *I Canoni Penali,* p. 72; Augustine, *A Commentary,* VIII, 317.

[34] Can. 2229, §§ 1, 3, 1o.

[35] Const. *"Quam plenum,"* § 4—*loc. cit.;* cf. Cippolini, *De Censuris,* p. 132; Cappello, *De Censuris,* n. 293, 3o; Pistocchi, *I Canoni Penali,* p. 72; Cerato, *Censurae Vigentes,* n. 54, nota; Cocchi, *Commentarium,* lib. V, n. 159, b.

The campaign against venality in ordinations and the Sacraments began very early,[36] and scarcely an age passed without some legislation upon such abuses.[37] With the promulgation of the Constitution "*Apostolicae Sedis,*" the *latae sententiae* penalties against simony in the administration of the sacraments and the conferring of Orders, were abrogated. The purpose of this Constitution was to limit the number of censures, and the penal law of the Church in this respect was to embrace only those expressly mentioned in the Constitution itself. The new Codification of the law has revived some of the old censures against abuses in the Sacraments.

§ 1. *The Subjects of the Law*

Four classes of persons are embraced by the law: 1. those who simoniacally confer orders; 2. those who thus receive orders; 3. those who simoniacally administer the Sacraments; and 4. those who thus receive the Sacraments. They *scienter* confer orders or administer the sacraments simoniacally, who without any lessening of imputability, either by an explicit or implicit, but at least externally manifested, agreement, bind themselves to the administration of the sacraments in return for some temporal good. Simoniacal reception consists in the rendering of some temporal advantage as a price of the sacrament received.[38] Here is involved only simony of the divine law.[39]

Many authors[40] contend that the word *scienter* applies both to the conferring and reception of orders and the abuse of the

---

[36] Council of Chalcedon, 451, c. 2—Hefele, *Conciliengeschichte,* II, 506; Council of Elvira, 300, c. 48—Hefele, *op. cit.,* I, 177.

[37] Chapter I of this dissertation; cf. Wernz, *Jus Decretalium,* VI, n. 342; Hinschius, *Kirchenrecht,* V, 162.

[38] Vermeersch-Creusen, *Epitome,* III, n. 574.

[39] Cocchi, *Commentarium,* lib. V, n. 244; Piscetta e Gennaro, *Elementa,* IV, n. 502, b; Cappello, *De Censuris,* n. 510, 2o; De Meester, *Compendium,* III, n. 1875; Cippolini, *De Censuris,* p. 208.

[40] Cappello, *De Censuris,* n. 510, 4o; Sole, *De Delictis et Poenis,* n. 429; Chelodi, *Jus Poenale,* n. 93; Pistocchi, *I Canoni Penali,* p. 257; Cippolini, *De Censuris,* p. 208; Cocchi, *Commentarium,* lib. V, n. 244, c; Cerato, *Censurae Vigentes,* n. 121.

other sacraments as well. Hence, they say, full imputability is required and ignorance of the law or even of the penalty, will excuse, even though it might be crass or supine. It is worthy of note that no cogent reasons are advanced to substantiate this opinion. On the other hand, the very position of the word *scienter* and the grammatical construction of the canon would seem to indicate that the legislator wished to confine this limitation to the conferring and reception of orders. If the word *scienter* were intended to affect the entire canon, the more logical position for it would be just before the words *ad ordines promoverint*. The fact that the legislator has placed it between the substantive *ordines* and the verbs which govern *ordines* may be taken as an indication that full knowledge and imputability is required only in the abuse of orders. Hence crass or supine ignorance would not excuse in the abuse of the other sacraments.[41]

Affected ignorance does not excuse from the penalties of this canon.[41a] The opinion sponsored by some authors[41b] before the Code, which defended affected ignorance, must, in view of the present legislation, be abandoned. It was argued that wherever words implying presumption or full knowledge were employed, deliberation, pure malice and contempt of the law were required. One who affected ignorance, they said, showed some respect for the law, in as much as he pretended to be ignorant of it, and consequently such a one was excused from the penalty. The present law, however, expressly states that affected ignorance does not excuse. What would be the result if the simony were committed by a third party? If the recipient of the Orders or Sacraments were ignorant of the fact, or even if he were aware of it, provided he does not cooperate, he does not incur the censure.[42]

---

[41] Augustine, *A Commentary,* VIII, 446. C. 2229, § 3.

[41a] Can. 2229, § 1.

[41b] Ballerini-Palmieri, *Opus Theologicum Morale,* I, nn. 39, 51; VII, n. 101, Lugo, *De Fide,* disp. XX, sect. 6; d'Annibale, *Summula Theologiae Moralis,* I, n. 312, not. 72.

[42] Augustine, *A Commentary,* VIII, 445; Cippolini, *De Censuris,* p. 208.

§ 2. *Orders and the Other Sacraments*

The Sacraments of the New Law are not merely signs of sacred things, but they actually produce sanctifying grace in the souls of properly disposed recipients. It is manifest, therefore, that venality in their administration or reception falls within the category of simoniacal abuse. Special emphasis is laid upon the Sacrament of Orders, possibly because this sacrament is the more liable to abuse.

i. *The Sacrament of Orders*

The terms employed in the law are general and hence include both major and minor orders. The extension of the word *orders* has been the subject of heated controversy even after the promulgation of the new law. The legislator has not been as clear as might be hoped and Doctors are not quite agreed whether the canon embraces simply orders in the strictest sense, or whether first tonsure and the episcopate must be considered under the sanction. Cippolini[43] contends that the canon must be interpreted in its strict sense, arguing that both from the context and the very nature of things, neither tonsure nor the episcopate should be included. In his opinion bishops are excused from the suspension attached to the canon, and since no one but a bishop can consecrate another, it seems logical that the episcopate be exempted from the sanction. If the canon did apply to the episcopate, there would be no subject for the penalty, for neither the consecrator, who is a bishop, nor the consecrated, who after the crime would be a bishop, would incur the suspension. Furthermore, he argues, the term *cleric* does not include a prelate. But the eminent Doctor seems to have overlooked the penalty of suspicion of heresy which is incurred even by bishops, and hence the sanction is not entirely without a subject. In exempting first tonsure, the same author contends that a simple cleric receives no power of orders or jurisdiction, and since he cannot be suspended, again there would be no subject to incur the suspension. On the contrary,

[43] *De Censuris*, p. 208.

since the suspension is *generaliter lata,* and involves privation of office and benefice, both of which might be possessed by a simple cleric, it would seem that Cippolini's arguments are not entirely valid.[44] Opinion is sufficiently divided to render the law doubtful, and under the circumstances, both the episcopate and first tonsure are not to be considered within the scope of the present canon.[45] The act must be complete, i.e., the order must have been conferred before the penalties are incurred, even though the price has not been paid, or perhaps never will be paid, provided only an agreement has been made.[46]

ii. *The Other Sacraments*

Besides the Sacrament of Orders, the penalties are incurred by traffic in the other sacraments, with the possible exception of the Sacrament of Matrimony.[47] It would be hard to conceive a simoniacal marriage, for the priest is merely a witness, the ministers of the sacrament being the parties themselves. Were the priest to charge for the nuptial blessing, while he would be guilty of simony, he would not incur the penalties laid down in the present canon, for the law does not extend to simony in the sacramentals. In reference to the administration of the sacraments, the conclusion of Pistocchi[48] is not entirely correct. He says: "I laici possono essere fra coloro che ricevono Sacramenti non fra coloro che li conferiscono. . . ." A layman can be the extraordinary minister of baptism and it does not seem just to exempt him from incurring the suspicion of heresy for a delinquency condemned in the present canon. The case can

[44] Farrugia (*Commentarium in Censuras,* n. 331, b) excludes tonsure on the score that the canon refers to *clerici,* or those who have already received tonsure. However, in view of the fact that the order must be conferred before the penalties are incurred, even those who receive first tonsure are *clerici* in the sense of the Code. Cf. Cappello, *De Censuris,* n. 510; Cerato, *Censurae Vigentes,* n. 121; Sole, *De Delictis et Poenis,* n. 429; Pistocchi, *I Canoni Penali,* p. 257; Noldin, *De Censuris,* n. 119.

[45] "In poenis benignior est interpretatio facienda."—can. 2219, § 1; cf. Cappello, *loc. cit.,* n. 510; De Meester, *Compendium,* III, n. 1875.

[46] Augustine, *A Commentary,* VIII, 445; Cappello, *De Censuris,* n. 510, 3o.

[47] Blat, *Commentarium,* lib. V, n. 213.

[48] *I Canoni Penali,* p. 257.

become practical when no one can be found to administer baptism to a dying child, except one who demands a price for his service.

Since the canon expressly mentions the sacraments, simony in the sacramentals does not come within the scope of the present sanction.[49] Hence one who charged for the blessing of an abbot, while he would commit simony, would not incur the penalties. There is, of course, no simony involved if a temporal gift is received or even demanded on the occasion of the administration of the sacraments, where such is permitted by law or legitimate custom.[50] The temporal here is given not as a price of the spiritual, but rather as a means of sustenance for the minister or in recompense for some extrinsic labor connected with the functions.[51]

Would the subject be permitted to cooperate materially in the simony of another, who would absolutely refuse to administer a sacrament without receiving pay? The opinion of St. Thomas[52] seems to be somewhat harsh and stringent. In speaking of a priest's refusal to administer the sacrament of baptism without receiving pay for his services, the Angelic Doctor writes: "But if it were an adult in danger of death that wished to be baptized, and the priest were unwilling to baptize him without being paid, . . . if he is unable to have recourse to another, he must by no means pay a price for Baptism, and should rather die without being baptized, because for him the baptism of desire would supply the lack of the sacrament." Nevertheless, everyone has a right to the sacraments, especially those which are necessary as a means to salvation, and the payment of the price would not be for the sacrament, but for the removal of unjust opposition. Provided there is a grave

---

[49] Can. 2219, § 2; Cappello, *De Censuris*, n. 511; Cerato, *Censurae Vigentes*, n. 121, ad 1; Eichmann, *Das Strafrecht des Codex J.C.*, n. 80.

[50] Can. 730.

[51] Cf. Chapter IV. Those who demand more than what is allowed by diocesan statute or legitimate custom, besides being bound to restitution, are to be punished by heavy fines, and in case of relapse, are to be suspended or removed according to the gravity of their fault. Cf. Can. 2408.

[52] *Summa Theologica*, 2, 2, q. 100, a. 2, ad 1.

reason for the reception of the sacrament, e.g., the paschal precept or danger of death, it would not be simony to pay for the removal of this opposition[53] nor would one incur guilt for permitting another to sin in such circumstances.[54] Accordingly if the recipient were a cleric, he would not incur the suspension imposed by this canon.

§ 3. *The Penalties*

Those who traffic in the Sacraments, even though they are Bishops, are suspected of heresy. Clerics, in addition are to be suspended for such abuses. Authors are quite agreed upon the interpretation and application of the first penalty. The suspension has been the subject of much controversy. Before entering upon a discussion of the various opinions concerning the question, it might be well to examine in detail the nature of the suspicion of heresy.

i. *Suspicion of Heresy*

The scope of this penalty is very broad, including both clerics and laymen, Bishops and other clerics. Here one can see a reflection of the opinions of ancient writers, wherein simony was referred to as a heresy. Delinquents are to be admonished by the Ordinary of their condition.[55] The admonition here is juridic rather than paternal, i.e., it is the command of a superior made in virtue of his power of jurisdiction, and demanding or forbidding some act under penalty of canonical punishment.[56] It is not necessary that the Ordinary make the admonition personally; he may do so through another person, or even by the public mails, but in the latter case he should make sure that he secure a receipt to prove delivery of his letter.[57] If the person

---

[53] Noldin, *Summa Theologiae Moralis,* II, n. 196, b; Genicot, *Institutiones Theologiae Moralis,* I, n. 288, 3o; Cippolini, *De Censuris,* p. 209.

[54] St. Alphonsus, *Theologia Moralis,* lib. III, n. 103.

[55] Can. 2315. Cf. Blat, *Commentarium,* V, n. 140, 1o.

[56] Cappello, *De Censuris,* n. 218, 2o.

[57] Can. 2307, 2309, § 2; cf. Cappello, *loc. cit.,* n. 218, 3°; Chelodi, *Jus Poenale,* n. 55; Augustine, *A Commentary,* VII, 169.

refuses to accept the letter, or hinders in any way its delivery, he does not escape the penalty.[58] If after being admonished, he continues under the suspicion, the law provides various penalties.[59]. He is to be forbidden the exercise of any ecclesiastical legal acts, such as those of administrator of ecclesiastical property, judge, auditor, relator, *defensor vinculi,* promotor of justice and promotor of the faith (for beatification and canonization), courier, lawyer and proxy, sponsor at Baptism and Confirmation, active voice or right of voting at ecclesiastical elections, including those held by monastic chapters and chapters of religious communities, and acts of actual (not habitual) exercise of the *juspatronatus.*[60] After a second warning, a cleric must be suspended *a divinis* for failure to remove the suspicion. If, within six months from the infliction of this punishment, he has not made amends, he is to be considered a heretic, amenable to the penalties set forth in can. 2314. Continued persistence constitutes a presumption *juris et de jure* of heresy.[61]

ii. *The Suspension*

In addition to being suspected of heresy, clerics incur suspension reserved to the Holy See. Though a cleric is defined by the Code as one who has received first tonsure,[62] controversy is quite marked concerning the scope of the word in the present text. It would seem that bishops must be included, for the tenor of the canon is most severe and should embrace all who are not laics. Furthermore, first tonsure is a necessary basis of the episcopate. It would seem also that the antithesis is not cleric and bishop, but rather cleric and laic. Augustine[63] argues from the citation of bishops in the first part of the canon that it is quite clear that the legislator wished to include them in the

---

[58] Augustine, *loc. cit.*

[59] Can. 2315.

[60] Can. 2256, § 2.

[61] Cappello, *De Censuris,* n. 221, 3o.

[62] Can. 108, § 1.

[63] *A Commentary,* VIII, 447; cf. Noldin, *De Censuris,* n. 118; Eichmann, *Das Strafrecht,* n. 81.

suspension. He appeals to former legislation[64] as a proof that the mind of the Church has ever been to punish those who had been abusing their episcopal office in these shameful abuses. Moreover, he argues the absurdity and injustice of the exemption, since the greater culprit would be visited with lesser punishment.

However, though it must be admitted that bishops are clerics essentially, and are more opposed to laics in the antithesis than mere clerics, nevertheless, in law they do not come under the title of clerics in relation to other clerics.[65] Moreover, the text of the canon cannot be advanced as proof of their inclusion, because in the first part of the text they are expressly mentioned, and in the latter half where the censure is inflicted, no mention is made of them.[66] Their preeminence is rather an argument in favor of their exclusion, since on this account the crime could not be as easily concealed. Suspicion of heresy and the consequent penalties, seem to be sufficient. The fact that they were included under the old law is no argument that the legislator wished them to be embraced by the new.[67] Greater guilt is explicitly stated to be no reason for the extension of a penalty.[68] Since they are not expressly mentioned in the part of the canon which inflicts the suspension, it would seem that the legislator did not wish to include them.[69] This exemption is confined to residential bishops and titulars and does not include Abbots Regular, Abbots and Prelates *nullius* and others who, although they have power to confer minor orders, are not consecrated bishops.[70] Since Cardinals are exempt from the penal laws of the Church, unless expressly mentioned, they too are not embraced by the present sanction.[71]

[64] C. 6, 8, 101, 107, 113, C. I, q. 1; c. 4, C. II, q. 5; c. 4, 5, 11, 13, X, *de simonia,* V, 3.

[65] Cippolini, *De Censuris,* p. 207.

[66] Cappello, *De Censuris,* n. 510; Kober, *Der Kirchenbann,* p. 200; Pistocchi, *I Canoni Penali,* p. 257; Chelodi, *Jus Poenale,* n. 93; Cocchi, *Commentarium,* lib. V, n. 244, d.

[67] Can. 6, 3o.

[68] Can. 2219, § 2.

[69] Can. 2227, § 2.

[70] Cappello, *De Censuris,* n. 510.

[71] Can. 2227, § 2.

Though still severe, it should be noted that the present legislation is more lenient than was the former discipline which inflicted excommunication upon those guilty of abuses in Holy Orders. Suspension deprives the subject of the rights to his office or benefice or both, but it does not necessarily take from him the offices or benefices themselves.[72] It affects all the benefices and offices which a cleric holds within the jurisdiction of the superior who suspends him, the powers of the superior being territorial.[73] Thus, if a cleric is suspended by a bishop, he loses his rights to all benefices and offices within the territory of that bishop, not however those which he may hold in another diocese.[74] On the other hand, when the suspension is *latae sententiae,* inflicted by the common law, it affects all benefices and offices, no matter in what territory the suspended person may hold them, as is true in the present canon. Since the penalty is not limited in any way by appended clauses, it is understood to be a general one, carrying all the effects of both suspension from office and suspension from benefice.[75]

Article III.—Offices, Benefices and Dignities

Canon 2392.—Firmo praescripto can. 729, delictum perpetrantes simoniae in quibuslibet officiis, beneficiis aut dignitatibus ecclesiasticis:

1°. Incurrunt in excommunicationem latae sententiae Sedi Apostolicae simpliciter reservatam;

2°. Ipso facto privati in perpetuum manent jure eligendi, praesentandi, nominandi, si quod habeant;

3°. Si clerici sint, praeterea suspendantur.

As has been stated above,[76] canon 729 renders null and void any simoniacal provision of offices, benefices or dignities, with

---

[72] Cappello, *De Censuris,* n. 495, c; Schmalzgrueber, *Jus Ecclesiasticum Universum,* lib. V, tit. XXXIX, n. 265; Wernz, *loc. cit.,* n. 208; Augustine, *A Commentary,* VIII, 220.

[73] Can. 2281.

[74] Can. 2282.

[75] Can. 2278; cf. Cappello, *De Censuris,* n. 511; Cippolini, *De Censuris,* p. 209; Augustine, *A Commentary,* VIII, 447.

[76] Chapter III.

the exception of the Papal election.[77] Moreover those guilty of simony in the acquisition of offices, benefices or dignities incur *ipso facto* excommunication reserved in a simple manner to the Holy See. In addition, they are deprived forever of their right of electing, presenting or nominating, and if they are clerics, they are to be suspended. It might seem curious that, for what apparently is a greater crime, namely simony in the administration of the Sacraments, the punishment is lesser in degree and intensity.[78] But the inducements for traffic in benefices are greater than for abuses of the Sacraments, because of the temporal advantages which are connected with the possession of these offices. Hence, threats of graver punishment are needed in order to deter the avaricious from traffic in benefices.[79]

Express mention is made of a *delictum*. Hence the crime should be external and morally imputable,[80] as well as complete, according to the text of the canons.[81] To incur the censure, it must be established that the bribe or price was offered and accepted, or at least an illicit contract was made.[82] Where the agreement is only implicit, there is necessary a transfer of the object of the contract by at least one of the parties, otherwise, the simoniacal intention would not be manifested, nor would it be possible to judge its real character.[83]

In view of canon 728, the sanction of the present canon applies to conventional, confidential and real simony.[84] In the legislation preceding the Code, special mention was made of real simony in connection with benefices. In the present law, no such distinction is made, and since the codifiers were cognizant of the former laws, it is only logical to conclude that their

[77] Can. 145, § 1; cf. Article IV of this chapter.

[78] Can. 2371; cf. Article II of this chapter.

[79] The nature of the office, benefice and dignity, and the various methods of committing simony therein, have been examined in detail in Chapter III.

[80] Can. 2195.

[81] Can. 2228.

[82] Augustine, *A Commentary*, VIII, 96.

[83] Cocchi, *Commentarium*, lib. V, n. 274, e.

[84] See above, chapter I, art. III.

silence on this point is an indication of their desire to embrace all species of simony under the present canon.[85]

All illicit transactions concerning election, presentation, designation, collation, institution, confirmation, possession, resignation, deduction of revenues, reservation of pensions, exchange of benefices without the consent of the Ordinary, are considered simony and are punished accordingly.[86] The object of the canon extends to all ecclesiastical offices in the strict sense, all benefices and dignities. Offices in a wider sense, such as professor, organist, sexton, procurator, etc., do not come within the scope of the present law.[87]

Since the crime must be complete (*perpetrantes*), the penalties are not incurred by merely attempted or frustrated violations of the law.[88] Such attempts, however, can be punished by the Ordinary, unless the person has freely and willingly desisted, and no damage nor scandal has been caused.[89] Cappello excuses those who enter upon a simoniacal contract, but for some reason, either voluntarily or involuntarily, cannot bring it to its desired conclusion.[90] However, since conventional simony is embraced by the law, the crime could be complete when the contract had been agreed to by both parties. It is not necessary that the conditions of the contract be fulfilled.[91] The authorities[92] quoted by Cappello wrote before the new codification when real simony was required by the law, and hence their opinions seem to lack probability in view of the clauses of the new law.

The penalty of excommunication is incurred by all clerics, including Bishops, with the exception of Cardinals, since the latter are not mentioned in the canon. Aspirants to offices,

---

[85] Augustine, *A Commentary*, VIII, 492; Cappello, *De Censuris*, n. 359, 7o; Cocchi, *Commentarium*, lib. V, n. 274, c; Chelodi, *Jus Poenale*, n. 104.

[86] See Chapter III. Cf. can. 185, 1435, 1465, § 2, 1470, § 1, 6o, 1441, 1486, 1927, § 1.

[87] Can. 145, § 2; Cocchi, *Commentarium*, lib. V, n. 274; Cippolini, *De Censuris*, p. 162.

[88] Can. 2212.

[89] Can. 2235, 2213.

[90] *De Censuris*, n. 360.

[91] Can. 728.

[92] Suarez, Schmalzgrueber, Pennacchi.

benefices and dignities, collators, electors and patrons, possessors or titulars in the case of resignations, and even disinterested persons wishing to secure these offices for another, all come within the scope of this canon.[93] Besides incurring excommunication, those possessing the right of electing, nominating or presenting candidates, are deprived of this right forever. Are they deprived of the right to be elected, nominated or presented to the benefice? Pius V, in his constitution *Cum primum,*[94] expressly declared that those who were guilty of simony in benefices or ecclesiastical offices were ineligible, not only for the position they sought to buy, but also for any other benefices. A custom derogating from this law seems to have arisen, which secured legitimate prescription, to the effect that simoniacs were eligible for offices other than the one they desired to purchase. Accordingly, unless the crime had been sentenced in court, no dispensation was required from ineligibility for benefices other than the one which was tainted with simony.[95] Since this irregularity was not a censure, it remained in force even after the promulgation of the constitution *"Apostolicae Sedis,"* for the latter concerned itself only with the abrogation of censures. The tenor of canon 6, 5° is restrictive of penal legislation. Only those penalties mentioned in the Code are considered to be still in force. Hence, the silence of canon 2392 upon the matter of ineligibility for offices in the case of simony, can be taken as an indication that this penalty was abolished by the Code.

Clerics, guilty of simony in the acquisition of benefices, offices and dignities, are to be suspended. Although the excommunication and privation of electoral rights are incurred by the very act of commission of the crime, the suspension is *ferendae sententiae.* The penalty, however, is couched in preceptive terms and hence its application is not left to the discretion of the Ordinary. Certain things are left to his good judgment.[96] He may defer inflicting the suspension, if he foresees that a greater evil will follow from it. Omission of the punishment

[93] Cocchi, *Commentarium,* lib. V, n. 265, a.

[94] 1 apr. 1556—*Fontes,* n. 111.

[95] Suarez, *Opera Omnia,* tom. XIII, lib. IV, c. 58, n. 11.

[96] Can. 2223, § 3.

entirely is allowed, if the guilty one has made amends and repaired the scandal, or if he has been punished sufficiently or will be punished by civil sanctions. The Bishop may mitigate the punishment specified in the law, or use in its stead one of the penal remedies, if there are circumstances present which would diminish the imputability in a notable degree. Since Bishops are excluded only from *latae sententiae* suspensions and interdicts, this suspension can be inflicted upon them, but by the Sovereign Pontiff alone.[97]

ARTICLE IV.—THE PAPAL ELECTION

Canon 2330.—Quod attinet ad poenas statutas in delicta quae in eligendo Summo Pontifice committi possunt, unice standum const. Pii X *Vacante Sede Apostolica*, 25 Dec. 1904.

Simoniae crimen, tam divino quam humano jure detestabile, in electione Romani Pontificis omnino sicut reprobatum esse constat, ita et Nos reprobamus atque damnamus, huiusque criminis reos poena excommunicationis latae sententiae innodamus; sublata tamen irritatione electionis simoniacae, quam Deus avertat, a Iulio II (vel alio qualicumque decreto pontificio) statuta, ut praetextus amputetur impugnandi valorem electionis Romani Pontificis. (n. 79) . . . ita ut hanc legem violantes . . . a nullo, ne a Maiori quidem Poenitentiario, cuiuslibet facultatis vigore, praeterquam a Romano Pontifice, nisi in mortis articulo, absolvi possint. (n. 51)—Const. "*Vacante Sede Apostolica*."[98]

---

[97] Can. 1557, § 1.

[98] A word of explanation might be in order concerning the extracts of the Constitution given above. Paragraph n. 79 states the penalty to be incurred by those who commit the crime of simony in the papal election. Somewhat previous to this paragraph, the Pontiff speaks of the violation of the secret of the Conclave. After establishing the penalty of excommunication for those who violate the secret, the Pope stated that not only this penalty, but every penalty of excommunication inflicted by the Constitution was reserved in a very special way personally to the Sovereign Pontiff. Although this reservation actually preceded the establishment of the punishment of simony in the Constitution, the writer thought it better to state the nature of the sanction first, and then add such excerpts from the preceding paragraph as would bring out clearly the character of the reservation.

The provisions of the common law relating to simoniacal elections do not refer to illicit transactions in papal elections. The latter have been removed from the provisions of the Code by canon 2330 and are to be governed entirely by the constitution *"Vacante Sede Apostolica,"* of Pius X, which is contained in the appendix to the Code. Until the time of the promulgation of this Constitution simoniacal elections to the papacy were invalid, and even under the common law today they would be invalid.[99] In order that the accusation of simony might not continue to furnish men with the pretext for attacking the validity of the election, Pius X saw fit to remove the invalidating clause from the law governing the choice of the Pontiff. Cippolini[100] restricts the provisions of the Constitution to simony of the divine law, on the ground that only such simony is a *crimen tam divino quam humano jure detestabile.* Simony of the ecclesiastical law is not, of necessity, contrary to divine law. Others,[101] however, extend the penalty to simony of the ecclesiastical law, without giving any cogent reasons for their opinion.

The penalty established by the Constitution must be restricted to simony concerning the election itself, and cannot be said to pertain to other secondary matters, e.g., the choosing of officials of the Conclave, nor to any mercenary attempts to win the favor of the Cardinal-electors, unless the latter might be equivalent to the purchase of votes. In other words, simony in the papal elections consists in any onerous contract in which the Cardinals' votes are bought or sold, or by which an obligation of temporal compensation is placed in exchange for the election. Stipulations for the increase of the Cardinals' *honorarium,* or obligations to confer upon them offices, benefices or dignities in return for their votes, would also fall within the scope of the censure. The excommunication would be incurred if the promise of a vote were made to a friend or relative of the nominee, on condition that he would use his influence with the new Pope

---

[99] Can. 729.

[100] *De Censuris,* p. 246.

[101] Chelodi, *Jus Poenale,* n. 68; Cappello, *De Censuris,* n. 571; Vermeersch-Creusen, *Epitome,* III, n. 530, 5º.

to secure some recompense for the elector. In all cases, however, there must be a true obligation placed upon the other party, for the hope of recompense would not suffice to constitute simony.

§ 1. *The Nature of the Censure*

The excommunication is *specialissimo modo* reserved to the Sovereign Pontiff, in such a way that it has been removed from the competence of the Major Penitentiary, except *in articulo mortis.* While there is a difference between the *articulo* and *periculo mortis,* there is practically the same necessity in both cases, and it is not very likely that the legislator wished to restrict the use of faculties until the very last moment.[102] Hence, it would seem that the faculties granted to all priests by canon 882, *in periculo mortis,* would apply also to this censure. Some authors[103] exempt the censure from the faculty given for urgent cases by the common law,[104] on the ground that the absolution is reserved exclusively to the Roman Pontiff except *in articulo mortis.* Others[105] argue, and it would seem rightly, that canon 2254, § 1, applies to all censures, no matter how they are reserved, and includes also the censures contained in the constitution in question. The Sovereign Pontiff, in casting the law, had in mind, apparently, ordinary circumstances, and not the extraordinary conditions mentioned in canon 2254. The obligation of recourse to the superior would still remain, unless moral impossibility excused from it. In this connection, it should be noted that such recourse can be made only to the Pope himself, for he alone is the Superior endowed with faculties, required by the canon.

§ 2. *The Subject of the Censure*

The constitution inflicts censure upon all those guilty of the crime of simony in the election. Hence, not only those who sell their votes, but also those who pay for the election come under

---

[102] Cippolini, *De Censuris,* p. 237.

[103] Cerato, *Censurae Vigentes,* n. 85; Pistocchi, *I Canoni Penali,* p. 76.

[104] Can. 2254.

[105] Cippolini, *De Censuris,* p. 238; Chelodi, *Jus Poenale,* n. 68; Cappello, *De Censuris,* n. 565, 2o.

this sanction. The question naturally arises concerning the exemption of Cardinals. According to canon 19, those laws which inflict a penalty or restrict the free exercise of rights, or contain an exception to the law, must be interpreted strictly. In case of doubt, the more lenient interpretation is to be followed.[106] The privilege of exemption from penal laws is accorded to Cardinals, unless they are expressly mentioned and there is no such reference made in the paragraph of the constitution which refers to simony.[107] Some authors[108] contend that Cardinals are included under the censure, in as much as the constitution of Julius II, "*Cum tam divino,*" upon which the constitution of Pius X is based, mentioned cardinals as the subjects of the penalty. Canon 2227, they say, cannot be applied here, since the Code expressly says that matters pertaining to papal elections are to be governed exclusively by the constitution "*Vacante Sede Apostolica.*" Blat,[109] on the other hand, interprets the word *unice* to mean that the penalties are to be drawn from the "*Vacante Sede Apostolica,*" to the exclusion of other constitutions on the same matter. Does the privilege of exemption given to Cardinals by the Code extend to the documents appended to the Code, or is the papal election controlled entirely by the constitution? In view of the diversity of opinion and the delicate nature of the question, the present writer will content himself with humbly repeating the words of Cappello:[110] "Nostram sententiam proferre non audemus. Videant sapientiores."

---

[106] Can. 2219, § 1.

[107] Const. "*Vacante Sede Apostolica,*" § 79.

[108] Vermeersch-Creusen, *Epitome,* III, n. 530, 5o; Farrugia, *Commentarium in Censuras,* n. 280.

[109] *Commentarium,* lib. V, n. 171.

[110] *De Censuris,* n. 571, 3o.

BIBLIOGRAPHY

Sources

Acta Apostolicae Sedis (*AAS*), Romae, 1909—

Acta et Decreta Conciliorum Recentiorum (*Collectio Lacensis*), 7 vols., Friburgi Brisgoviae, 1870-1890.

Acta Sanctae Sedis (*ASS*), 41 vols., Romae, 1865-1908.

Benedicti Papae XIV Bullarium, 13 vols., Mechlinae, 1826-1827.

Bullarium Diplomatum et Privilegiorum Sanctorum Pontificum Taurinensis Editio, 24 vols., Augustae Taurinorum, 1857-1872.

Canones et Decreta Concilii Tridentini, 19 ed., Taurini, 1913.

Codex Juris Canonici Pii X Pontificis Maximi jussu digestus Benedicti Papae XV auctoritate promulgatus, Romae, 1918.

Codicis Juris Canonici Fontes, cura Emi. Petri Card. Gasparri editi, 5 vols., Romae, 1925-1930.

Collectanea in Usum Secretariae S. C. Episcoporum et Regularium, ed. A. Bizzarri, Romae, 1885.

Collectanea S. Congregationis de Propaganda Fide, 2 vols., Romae, 1907.

Concilii Plenarii Baltimorensis II (1868), Acta et Decreta, Baltimorae, 1868.

Concilii Plenarii Baltimorensis III (1884), Acta et Decreta, Baltimorae, 1886.

Corpus Juris Canonici, Editio Lipsiensis II (Richter-Friedberg), 2 vols., Lipsiae, 1922.

Corpus Juris Civilis, ed. P. Krueger, Berolini, 1922.

Ghilardi, J., *Epitome Canonum Conciliorum tum Generalium tum Provincialium ab Apostolis usque ad Annum MDCIX*, 2 vols, Monteregali, 1870.

Mansi, Joannes, *Sacrorum Conciliorum Nova et Amplissima Collectio*, 53 vols., Parisiis, 1901-1927.

Migne, Jacques, *Patrologiae Cursus Completus,—Series Latina*, 221 vols., *(MPL)*, Parisiis, 1844-1855; *Series Graeca*, 161 vols., *(MPG)*, Parisiis, 1858-1864.

Syndicon Orientale ou Recueil des Synodes Nestoriens, (Chabot), Paris, 1902.

Thesaurus Resolutionum Sacrae Congregationis Concilii, 167 vols., Romae, 1718-1908.

WORKS OF REFERENCE

Alphonsus, De Liguori, *Theologia Moralis,* 5 vols., Taurini, 1872.

Alzog, J., *Manual of Universal Church History,* 3 vols., translated by F. J. Pabisch and Thos. S. Byrne, Cincinnati, 1876.

Ansillon, J., *De Simonia et Munerum ac Retributionum Gratificatione in Re Beneficiaria,* Leodii, 1677.

Augustine, Charles, *A Commentary on the New Code of Canon Law,* 2 ed., 8 vols., St. Louis, 1921-1924.

Ayrinhac, H. A., *Constitution of the Church in the New Code of Canon Law,* New York, 1925.

Ayrinhac, H. A., *Penal Legislation in the New Code of Canon Law,* New York, 1920.

Ballerini-Palmieri, *Opus Theologicum Morale,* 7 vols., Prati, 1890.

Benedictus XIV, *Tractatus de Missae Sacrificio,* Mechlinae, 1860.

Bigg, Charles, *The Origins of Christianity,* Oxford, 1909.

Bingham, Joseph, *Antiquities of the Christian Church,* 2 vols., London, 1856.

Blat, Albertus, *Commentarium Textus Codicis Juris Canonici,* 5 vols., Romae, 1921-1927.

Bonacina, Martinus, *Opera Omnia,* 3 vols., Venetiis, 1686.

Bright, Wm., *Notes on the Canons of the First Four General Councils,* Oxford, 1882.

Burke, F. J., *Characteristics of the Early Church,* Baltimore, 1889.

Cajetanus, Thomasso de Vio, *Opuscula Omnia,* Lugduni, 1585.

Cappello, Felix, *Tractatus Canonico-Moralis de Censuris juxta Codicem Juris Canonici,* 2 ed., Taurinorum Augustae, 1925.

Cappello, Felix, *Tractatus Canonico-Moralis de Sacramentis juxta Codicem Juris Canonici,* 3 vols., Taurinorum Augustae, 1927.

Cardini, Emidio, *Dei Supremi Principi della Teologia Morale Studi,* 5 vols., Fierenze, 1891.

Cerato, P., *Censurae Vigentes Ipso Facto a Codice Juris Canonici Excerptae,* 2 ed., Patavii, 1921.

Chelodi, Joannes, *Jus de Personis juxta Codicem Juris Canonici,* 2 ed., Tridenti, 1927.

Chelodi, Joannes, *Jus Poenale et Ordo Procedendi in Judiciis criminalibus juxta Codicem Juris Canonici,* Tridenti, 1925.

Claeys-Bouuaert-Simenon, *Manuale Juris Canonici,* 2 ed., Bandae et Leodii, 1926.

Cippolini, Albertus, *De Censuris Latae Sententiae juxta Codicem Juris Canonici,* Taurini, 1925.

Cocchi, Guidus, *Commentarium in Codicem Juris Canonici,* 2 and 3 ed., 8 vols., 1925-1930.

Concina, Daniel, *Theologia Christiana Dogmatico-Moralis,* 10 vols., Neapoli, 1772.

Cornelius a Lapide, *Commentarium in Epistolas Canonicas,* Venetiis, 1717.

D'Annibale, Josephus, *In Constitutionem "Apostolicae Sedis" qua Censurae Latae Sententiae Limitantur Commentarii*, Romae, 1909.

D'Annibale, Josephus, *Summula Theologiae Moralis*, Romae, 1897.

De Ledesma, Petrus, *Theologia Moralis*, Tornaci, 1636.

De Meester, A., *Juris Canonici et Juris Canonico-Civilis Compendium*, 2 ed., 3 vols., Brugis, 1921-1928.

Denziger, H., *Enchiridion Symbolorum et Definitionum*, 9 ed., Lipsiae, 1900.

De Panormo, Antonius, *Scrutinium Doctrinarum*, Romae, 1709.

De Pressense, E., *The Early Years of Christianity*, translated by Harwood-Holmden, 6 ed., London, 1889.

Deshayes, P., *Memento Juris Publici et Privati*, Paris, 1895.

Devoti, Joannes, *Institutionum Canonicarum Editio Prima post Quintam*, 5 vols., Romae, 1826.

Dictionnaire d' Archeologie Chretienne et de Liturgie, ed. F. Cabrol, Paris, 1924.

Duchesne, J., *The Early History of the Christian Church*, New York, 1909.

Durandus, Gulielmus, *Speculum Juris*, 3 vols., Venetiis, 1586.

Edmundson, Geo., *The Church in Rome in the First Century*, London, 1913.

Eichmann, Eduard, *Das Strafrecht des Codex Juris Canonici*, Paderborn, 1920.

Fanfani, Ludovicus, *De Jure Parochorum ad Norman Codicis Juris Canonici*, Taurini-Romae.

Farrugia, Nicholaus, *Commentarium Milevitanum in Censuras Latae Sententiae Codicis Juris Canonici*, Melitae, 1919.

Ferraris, Lucius, *Bibliotheca canonica juridica moralis theologica nec non ascetica polemica rubricistica historica*, 9 vols., Romae, 1889.

Ferreres, Joannes, *Compendium Theologiae Moralis*, 7 ed., 2 vols., Barcinone, 1928.

Ferreres, Joannes, *Institutiones Canonicae juxta Novissimum Codicem Pii X a Benedicto XV promulgatum juxtaque praescripta Hispanae Disciplinae et Americae Latinae*, 2 vols., Barcinone, 1918.

Ferry, Wm., *Stole Fees*, Washington, 1930.

Fleury, C., *Ecclesiastical History*, translated with notes by J. H. Newman, 2 vols., London, 1844.

Fowler, M., *Christian Egypt*, London, 1901.

Funk, F. X., *A Manual of Church History*, translated from the 5th. German edition by Luigi Cappadelta, 2 vols., St. Louis, 1910.

Garcia, Nicholas, *Tractatus de beneficiis amplissimus et doctissimus*, Coloniae Allobrogum, 1636.

Gasparri, P., *Tractatus Canonicus de SS. Eucharistia*, 2 vols., Parisiis, 1897.

Gasquet, Abbot, *Parish Life in Mediaeval England*, New York, 1906.

Genicot-Salsmans, *Institutiones Theologiae Moralis*, 10 ed., 2 vols., Bruxellis, 1922.

Gennari, Casmirus, *Consultazioni Morali-Canoniche-Liturgiche su casi e materie svariate*, 2 vols., Romae, 1895.

Gibalinus, J., *De Simonia Universa Tractatio Theologica et Canonica*, Lugduni, 1659.

Golden, Henry Francis, *Parochial Benefices in the New Code*, Washington, 1925.

Gonzalez, E., *Commentaria Perpetua in Singulos Textus Quinque Librorum Decretalium Gregorii IX*, 3 vols., Venetiis, 1699.

Grisar, Hartmann, *Luther*, translated by E. M. Lamond, edited by Luigi Cappadelta, 6 vols., St. Louis, 1913-1917.

Hefele, Carl Joseph von, *Conciliengeschichte*, 2 ed., 9 vols., Freiburg, 1873-1890.

Hinschius, P., *System des katholischen Kirchenrechts*, vol. V, Berlin, 1895.

Josephus, Flavius, *Antiquitatum Judaicarum Libri XX*, Basileae, 1554.

Jaffé, Ph., Wattenbach, S., Loenwenfeld, F., Kaltenbrummer, F., Ewald, P., *Regesta Pontificum Romanorum*, 2 vols., Lipsiae, 1885-1888.

Keller, Charles, *Mass Stipends*, Washington, 1925.

Kenrick, F. P., *Theologia Moralis*, 2 ed., 2 vols., Mechlinae, 1841.

Kober, F., *Der Kirchenbann*, Tübingen, 1863.

Koch-Preuss, *A Handbook of Moral Theology*, 5 vols., St. Louis, 1921.

La Croix, Claudius, *Theologia Moralis*, 2 vols., Coloniae, 1719.

Laymann, Paulus, *Theologia Moralis*, Venetiis, 1719.

Leech, George Leo, *A Comparative Study of the Constitution "Apostolicae Sedis" and the "Codex Juris Canonici,"* Washington, 1922.

Lehmkuhl, Augustinus, *Theologia Moralis*, 11 ed., 2 vols., Friburgi Brisgoviae, 1915.

Leinz, A., *Die Simonie*, Freiburg, 1902.

Lessius, Leonardus, *De Justitia et Jure Caeterisque Virtutibus Cardinalibus*, 3 ed., Antwerpiae, 1612.

Maitland, S. R., *The Dark Ages*, edited by F. Stokes, M. A., 5 ed., London, 1890.

Maroto, P., *Institutiones Juris Canonici*, 3 ed., 2 vols., Romae, 1921.

Martin, Michael, *The Roman Curia as it Now Exists*, London, 1913.

McGiffert, A. C., *A History of Christianity in the Apostolic Age*, New York, 1903.

Moneta, J. P., *Tractatus de Distributionibus Quotidianis*, Romae, 1632.

Navarrus, M. A., *Opera Omnia*, 6 vols., Venetiis, 1621.

Newman, John Henry, *Historical Sketches*, 3 vols., London, 1896.

Newman, John Henry, *The Present Position of Catholics in England*, 2 ed., London, 1896.

Noldin, H., *Summa Theologiae Moralis*, 18 ed., 3 vols., Oeniponte, 1926.

Pastor, Ludwig von, *The History of the Popes from the Close of the Middle Ages*, edited by F. I. Antrobus, 18 vols., London, 1891.

Paulus, N., *Geschichte des Ablasses im Mittelalter*, 3 vols., Paderborn, 1922.

Pennacchi, J., *Commentaria in Constitutionem "Apostolicae Sedis,"* 2 vols., Romae, 1883.

Pichler, Vitus, *Jus Canonicum*, 2 vols., Ravennae, 1741.

Pighi, J. B., *Censurae Latae Sententiae*, Veronae, 1919.

Pirhing, Enricus, *Jus Canonicum Nova Methodo Explicatum*, 2 vols., Delingae, 1678.

Pistocchi, M., *I Canoni Penali del Codice Ecclesiastico Eposti e Commentati*, Torino, 1925.

Pistocchi, M., *De Re Beneficiali*, Taurini, 1928.

Pohle-Preuss, *The Sacraments*, vol. III, St. Louis, 1920.

Pruemmer, Dom., *Manuale Juris Canonici*, 4 et 5 ed., Friburgi Brisgoviae, 1927.

Pruemmer, Dom., *Manuale Theologiae Moralis*, 2 ed., 3 vols., Friburgi Brisgoviae, 1923.

Raymundus de Pennaforte, *Summa*, Veronae, 1744.

Reiffenstuel, Anacletus, *Jus Canonicum Universum*, 4 vols., Romae, 1838.

Rigantius, Josephus, *Commentarium in Regulas, Constitutiones et Ordinationes Cancellariae Apostolicae*, 4 vols. in 2, Coloniae Allobrogum, 1751.

Sabetti-Barrett, *Compendium Theologiae Moralis*, 22 ed., New York, 1915.

Salmanticenses, *Cursus Theologiae Moralis*, 3 vols., Venetiis, 1728.

Sanchez, Thomas, *Consilia seu Opuscula Moralia*, 2 vols., Antuerpiae, 1636.

Santi, Fr., *Praelectiones Juris Canonici*, 2 ed., 5 vols., Ratisbonne, 1892.

Scavini, Petrus, *Theologia Moralis Universa ad Mentem S. Alphonsi M. de Ligorio*, 11 ed., 4 vols., Mediolani, 1869.

Schäfer, Timotheus P., *Compendium de Religiosis ad Norman Codicis Juris Canonici*, Münster, 1927.

Schmalzgrueber, Franciscus, *Jus Ecclesiasticum Universum*, 12 vols., Romae, 1844.

Slater, Thomas, *Manual of Moral Theology with Notes on American Legislation*, 3 ed., 2 vols., New York, 1909.

Smith, S. B., *Elements of Ecclesiastical Law*, 3 vols., New York, 1887.

Sole, I., *De Delictis et Poenis*, Romae, 1920.

Soto, Dominicus, *De Justitia et Jure*, Salamanticae, 1556.

Suarez, Franciscus, *Opera Omnia*, 26 vols., Parisiis, 1856.

Tanquerey, Ad., *Synopsis Theologiae Dogmaticae*, 20 ed., 3 vols., Romae, 1926.

Tanquerey, Ad., *Synopsis Theologiae Moralis et Pastoralis ad mentem S. Thomae et S. Alphonsi Hodiernis Moribis Accomodata*, 8 ed., 3 vols., Romae, 1921.

Thomas Aquinas, *Summa Theologica*, 2 ed., Romae, 1894.

Thomassinus, L., *Vetus et Nova Ecclesiae Disciplina Circa Beneficia et Beneficiarios*, 10 vols., Maguntiae, 1787.

Ugolinus, Bartholomeus, *Tractatus de Simonia*, Venetiis, 1599.

Vermeersch-Creusen, *Epitome Juris Canonici cum Commentariis ad Scholas et ad Usum Privatum*, 2 et 3 ed., 3 vols., Romae, 1925-1927.

Vogt, Jos., *Das Kirchliche Vermögensrecht*, 2 ed., Cologne, 1910.

Waterworth, *Canons and Decrees of the Council of Trent*, London, 1848.

Weber, N. A., *A History of Simony in the Christian Church*, Baltimore, 1909.

Wernz, Franciscus, *Jus Decretalium ad Usum Praelectionum in Scholis Textus Canonici sive Juris Decretalium,* 6 vols., Prati, 1915.

Wernz-Vidal, *Jus Canonicum,* 3 vols., Romae, 1923-1927.

Wigran, W. A., *An Introduction to the History of the Assyrian Church,* London, 1910.

Zallinger, J. A., *Institutiones Juris Ecclesiastici,* 5 vols., Romae, 1823.

PERIODICALS

American Ecclesiastical Review, The (AER), Philadelphia, 1889.

Archiv für katholisches Kirchenrecht (Ak K R), Innsbruck, 1857.

Catholic World, The, New York, 1865.

Dublin Review, The, Dublin, 1836.

Il Monitore Ecclesiastico, Romae, 1888.

Irish Ecclesiastical Record (IER), Dublin, 1864.

Month, The, London, 1864.

Nouvelle Revue Theologique, Paris, 1856.

Periodica, de Re Canonica et Morali, Romae et Brugis, 1905.

Revue Benedictine, Abbaye de Maredsous, 1884.

Zeitschrift für katholische Theologie, Innsbruck, 1877.

Universitas Catholica Americae

Washington, D. C.

Facultas Iuris Canonici

1931

No. 65

DEUS LUX MEA

TITULI

QUOS

AD DOCTORATUS GRADUM

IN

JURE CANONICO

APUD UNIVERSITATEM CATHOLICAM AMERICAE

CONSEQUENDUM

PUBLICE PROPUGNABIT

RAYMUNDUS A. RYDER

SACERDOS ARCHIDIOECESIS PHILADELPHIENSIS

JURIS CANONICI LICENTIATUS

HORA XI, A. M. DIE XXVII MAII MCMXXXI.

TITULI

IN IURE CANONICO

I.	De Dissertatione.	
II.	De Historia Iuris Canonici.	
III.	Canones 1-7	De Ambitu Codicis.
IV.	Canones 8-24	De Legibus Ecclesiasticis.
V.	Canones 25-30	De Consuetudine.
VI.	Canones 31-35	De Temporis Supputatione.
VII.	Canones 36-62	De Rescriptis.
VIII.	Canones 63-79	De Privilegiis.
IX.	Canones 80-86	De Dispensationibus.
X.	Canones 87-107	Generales Notiones de Personis.
XI.	Canones 111-117	De Clericorum Adscriptione Alicui Dioecesi.
XII.	Canones 118-123	De Iuribus et Privilegiis Clericorum.
XIII.	Canones 124-144	De Obligationibus Clericorum.
XIV.	Canones 145-195	De Officiis Ecclesiasticis.
XV.	Canones 196-210	De Potestate Ordinaria et Delegata.
XVI.	Canones 487-498	De Notione Religionis, et de Erectione et Suppressione Religionis, Provinciae, Domus.
XVII.	Canones 499-537	De Religionum Regimine.
XVIII.	Canones 538-586	De Admissione in Religionem.
XIX.	Canones 673-681	De Societatibus sive Virorum sive Mulierum in Communi Viventium sine Votis.
XX.	Canones 1012-1018	De Matrimonio in Genere.
XXI.	Canones 1019-1034	De Iis quae Matrimonii Celebrationi Praemitti debent.
XXII.	Canones 1035-1057	De Impedimentis in Genere.
XXIII.	Canones 1058-1066	De Impedimentis Impedientibus.
XXIV.	Canones 1067-1080	De Impedimentis Dirimentibus.
XXV.	Canones 1081-1093	De Consensu Matrimoniali.
XXVI.	Canones 1552-1568	De Notione Iudicii et de Foro Competenti.
XXVII.	Canones 1569-1607	De Variis Tribunalium Gradibus et Speciebus.
XXVIII.	Canones 1608-1645	De Disciplina in Tribunalibus Servanda.
XXIX.	Canones 1646-1666	De Partibus in Causa.
XXX.	Canones 1667-1705	De Actionibus et Exceptionibus.
XXXI.	Canones 1706-1725	De Causae Introductione.

TITULI

XXXII.	Canones 1726-1746	De Litis Contestatione, de Litis Instantia, et de Interrogationibus Partibus in Iudicio Faciendis.
XXXIII.	Canones 1747-1836	De Probationibus.
XXXIV.	Canones 1837-1857	De Causis Incidentibus.
XXXV.	Canones 1858-1877	De Processus Publicatione, de Conclusione in Causa, de Causae Discussione, et de Sententia.
XXXVI.	Canones 1879-1891	De Appellatione.
XXXVII.	Canones 1902-1907	De Re Iudicata et de Restitutione in Integrum.
XXXVIII.	Canones 1960-1992	De Causis Matrimonialibus.
XXXIX.	Canones 2195-2198	De Natura Delicti eiusque Divisione.
XL.	Canones 2199-2211	De Imputabilitate Delicti, de Causis illam Aggravantibus vel Minuentibus, et de Iuridicis Delicti Effectibus.
XLI.	Canones 2212-2213	De Conatu Delicti.
XLII.	Canones 2214-2240	De Poenis in Genere.
XLIII.	Canones 2241-2285	De Poenis Medicinalibus seu de Censuris.
XLIV.	Canones 2286-2305	De Poenis Vindicativis.
XLV.	Canones 2306-2313	De Remediis Poenalibus et Poenitentiis.

IN IURE ROMANO

XLVI. The Periods of Roman Law.
XLVII. The Sources of Roman Law.
XLVIII. Personality.
XLIX. Slavery.
L. Citizenship.
LI. Patria Potestas.
LII. Personae in Manu.
LIII. Tutela et Cura.
LIV. Personae in Mancipio.
LV. Ownership.
LVI. De Obligationibus in Genere.
LVII. De Obligationibus Extra-Contractualibus.
LVIII. Furtum.
LIX. Damnum Injuria Datum.
LX. Injuria.

Vidit Facultas:

VALENTINUS T. SCHAAF, O.F.M., J.C.D., Vice-Decanus.
LUDOVICUS H. MOTRY, S.T.D., J.C.D., a Secretis.
FRANCISCUS J. LARDONE, S.T.D., J.U.D.

Vidit Rector Magnificus Universitatis:

JACOBUS HUGO RYAN, S.T.D., Ph.D., LL.D., Litt.D.

BIOGRAPHICAL NOTE

Raymond A. Ryder was born July 8, 1904, at Philadelphia, Pennsylvania. He attended St. Anne's Parochial School and St. Joseph's College, Philadelphia. His philosophical and theological studies were made at St. Charles Seminary, Overbrook, Pennsylvania, from which institution he received the degree of Bachelor of Arts. In the fall of 1929 he entered the Catholic University to pursue a graduate course of studies in Canon Law. He was ordained to the Holy Priesthood on May 29, 1930.

CATHOLIC UNIVERSITY OF AMERICA

CANON LAW STUDIES

1. Freriks, Rev. Celestine A., C.PP.S., J.C.D., Religious Congregations in Their External Relations, 121 pp., 1916.
2. Galliher, Rev. Daniel M., O.P., J.C.D., Canonical Elections, 117 pp., 1917.
3. Borkowski, Rev. Aurelius L., O.F.M., J.C.D., De Confraternitatibus Ecclesiasticis, 136 pp., 1918.
4. Castillo, Rev. Cayo, J.C.D., Disertacion Historico-canonica sobre la Potestad del Cabildo en Sede Vacante o Impedida del Vicario Capitular, 99 pp., 1919 (1918).
5. Kubelbeck, Rev. William J., S.T.B., J.C.D., The Sacred Penitentiaria and Its Relations to Faculties of Ordinaries and Priests, 129 pp., 1918.
6. Petrovits, Rev. Joseph J. C., S.T.D., J.C.D., The New Church Law on Matrimony, X-461 pp., 1919.
7. Hickey, Rev. John J., S.T.B., J.C.D., Irregularities and Simple Impediments in the New Code of Canon Law, 100 pp., 1920.
8. Klekotka, Rev. Peter J., S.T.B., J.C.D., Diocesan Consultors, 179 pp., 1920.
9. Wannenmacher, Rev. Francis, J.C.D., The Evidence in Ecclesiastical Procedure Affecting the Marriage Bond, 1920. (Not Printed.)
10. Golden, Rev. Henry Francis, J.C.D., Parochial Benefices in the New Code, IV-119 pp., 1921. (Printed 1925).
11. Koudelka, Rev. Charles J., J.C.D., Pastors, Their Rights and Duties According to the New Code of Canon Law, 211 pp., 1921.
12. Melo, Rev. Antonius, O.F.M., J.C.D., De Exemptione Regularium, X-188 pp., 1921.
13. Schaaf, Rev. Valentine Theodore, O.F.M., S.T.B., J.C.D., The Cloister, X-180 pp., 1921.
14. Burke, Rev. Thomas Joseph, S.T.B., J.C.D., Competence in Ecclesiastical Tribunals, IV-117 pp., 1922.
15. Leech, Rev. George Leo, J.C.D., A Comparative Study of the Constitution "Apostolicae Sedis" and the "Codex Juris Canonici," 179 pp., 1922.
16. Motry, Rev. Hubert Louis, S.T.D., J.C.D., Diocesan Faculties according to the Code of Canon Law, II-167 pp., 1922.
17. Murphy, Rev. George Lawrence, J.C.D., Delinquencies and Penalties in the Administration and the Reception of the Sacraments, IV-121 pp., 1923.

18. O'REILLY, REV. JOHN ANTHONY, S.T.B., J.C.D., Ecclesiastical Sepulture in the New Code of Canon Law, II-129 pp., 1923.
19. MICHALICKA, REV. WENCESLAS CYRILL, O.S.B., J.C.D., Judicial Procedure in Dismissal of Clerical Exempt Religious, 107 pp., 1923.
20. DARGIN, REV. EDWARD VINCENT, S.T.B., J.C.D., Reserved Cases According to the Code of Canon Law, IV-103 pp., 1924.
21. GODFREY, REV. JOHN A., S.T.B., J.C.D., The Right of Patronage According to the Code of Canon Law, 153 pp., 1924.
22. HAGEDORN, REV. FRANCIS EDWARD, J.C.D., General Legislation on Indulgences, II-154 pp., 1924.
23. KING, REV. JAMES IGNATIUS, J.C.D., The Administration of the Sacraments to Dying Non-Catholics, V-141 pp., 1924.
24. WINSLOW, REV. FRANCIS JOSEPH, A.F.M., J.C.D., Vicars and Prefects Apostolic, IV-149 pp., 1924.
25. CORREA, REV. JOSE SERVELION, S.T.L., J.C.D., La Potestad Legislativa de la Iglesia Catolica, IV-127 pp., 1925.
26. DUGAN, REV. HENRY FRANCIS, M.A., J.C.D., The Judiciary Department of the Diocesan Curia, 87 pp., 1925.
27. KELLER, REV. CHARLES FREDERICK, S.T.B., J.C.D., Mass Stipends, 167 pp., 1925.
28. PASCHANG, REV. JOHN LINUS, J.C.D., The Sacramentals According to the Code of Canon Law, 129 pp., 1925.
29. PIONTEK, REV. CYRILLUS, O.F.M., S.T.B., J.C.D., De Indulto Exclaustrationis necnon Saecularizationis, XIII-289 pp., 1925.
30. KEARNEY, REV. RICHARD JOSEPH, S.T.B., J.C.D., Sponsors at Baptism According to the Code of Canon Law, IV-127 pp., 1925.
31. BARTLETT, REV. CHESTER JOSEPH, A.M., LL.B., J.C.D., The Tenure of Parochial Property in the United States of America, V-108 pp., 1926.
32. KILKER, REV. ADRIAN JEROME, J.C.D., Extreme Unction, V-425 pp., 1926.
33. MCCORMICK, REV. ROBERT EMMETT, J.C.D., Confessors of Religious, VIII-266 pp., 1926.
34. MILLER, REV. NEWTON THOMAS, J.C.D., Founded Masses According to the Code of Canon Law, VII-93 pp., 1926.
35. ROELKER, REV. EDWARD G., S.T.D., J.C.D., Principles of Privilege According to the Code of Canon Law, XI-166 pp., 1926.
36. BAKALARCZYK, REV. RICHARDUS, M.I.C., J.U.D., De Novitiatu, VIII-208 pp., 1927.
37. PIZZUTI, REV. LAWRENCE, O.F.M., J.U.L., De Parochis Religiosis, 1927. (Not Printed.)
38. BLILEY, REV. NICHOLAS MARTIN, O.S.B., J.C.D., Altars According to the Code of Canon Law, XIX-132 pp., 1927.
39. BROWN, BRENDAN FRANCIS, A.B., LL.M., J.U.D., The Canonical Juristic Personality with Special Reference to its Status in the United States of America, V-212 pp., 1927.

40. Cavanaugh, Rev. William Thomas, C.P., J.U.D., The Reservation of the Blessed Sacrament, VIII-101 pp., 1927.
41. Doheny, Rev. William J., C.S.C., A.B., J.U.D., Church Property: Modes of Acquisition, X-118 pp., 1927.
42. Feldhaus, Rev. Aloysius H., C.PP.S., J.C.D., Oratories, IX-141 pp., 1927.
43. Kelly, Rev. James Patrick, A.B., J.C.D., The Jurisdiction of the Simple Confessor, X-208 pp., 1927.
44. Neuberger, Rev. Nicholas J., J.C.D., Canon 6 or the Relation of the Codex Juris Canonici to the Preceding Legislation, V-95 pp., 1927.
45. O'Keeffe, Rev. Gerald Michael, J.C.D., Matrimonial Dispensations, Powers of Bishops, Priests, and Confessors, VIII-232 pp., 1927.
46. Quigley, Rev. Joseph, A.M., A.B., J.C.D., Condemned Societies, 139 pp., 1927.
47. Zaplotnik, Rev. Ioannes Leo, J.C.D., De Vicariis Foraneis, X-142, 1927.
48. Duskie, Rev. John Aloysius, A.B., J.C.D., The Canonical Status of the Orientals in the United States, VIII-196 pp., 1928.
49. Hyland, Rev. Francis Edward, J.C.D., Excommunication, Its Nature, Historical Development and Effects, VIII-181 pp., 1928.
50. Reinmann, Rev. Gerald Joseph, O.M.C., J.C.D., The Third Order Secular of Saint Francis, 201 pp., 1928.
51. Schenk, Rev. Francis J., J.C.D., The Matrimonial Impediments of Mixed Religion and Disparity of Cult. XVI-318 pp., 1929.
52. Coady, Rev. John Joseph, S.T.D., J.U.D., A.M., The Appointment of Pastors, VIII-150 pp., 1929.
53. Kay, Rev. Thomas Henry, J.C.D., Competence in Matrimonial Procedure, VIII-164 pp., 1929.
54. Turner, Rev. Sidney Joseph, C.P., J.U.D., The Vow of Poverty, XLIX-217 pp., 1929.
55. Kearney, Rev. Raymond A., A.B., S.T.D., J.C.D., The Principles of Delegation, VII-149 pp., 1929.
56. Conran, Rev. Edward James, A.B., J.C.D., The Interdict, V-163 pp., 1930.
57. O'Neill, Rev. William H., J.C.D., Papal Rescripts of Favor, VII-219 pp., 1930.
58. Bastnagel, Rev. Clement Vincent, J.U.D., The Appointment of Parochial Adjutants and Assistants, XV-262 pp., 1930.
59. Ferry, Rev. William A., A.B., J.C.D., Stole Fees, X-108 pp., 1930.
60. Costello, Rev. John Michael, A.B., J.C.D., Domicile and Quasi-Domicile, VII-201 pp., 1930.
61. Kremer, Rev. Michael Nicholas, A.B., S.T.B., J.C.D., Church Support in the United States, VI-137 pp., 1930.
62. Angulo, Rev. Luis, C.M., J.C.L., Legislación de la Iglesia Católica sobre la Intención en la Aplicación de la Misa, 1931.

63. FREY, REV. WOLFGANG, O.S.B., A.B., J.C.L., The Act of Religious Profession, 1931.
64. ROBERTS, REV. JAMES BRENDAN, A.B., J.C.L., The Banns of Marriage, 1931.
65. RYDER, REV. RAYMOND ALOYSIUS, A.B., J.C.L., Simony, 1931.
66. CAMPAGNA, REV. MICHAEL ANGELO, Ph.B., J.U.L., Il Vicario Generale del Vescovo, 1931.
67. COX, REV. JOSEPH GODFREY, A.B., J.C.L., The Administration of Seminaries, 1931.
68. GREGORY, REV. DONALD JOSEPH, S.T.B., J.U.L., The Pauline Privilege, 1931.
69. DONOHUE, REV. JOHN FRANCIS, A.M., J.C.L., The Impediment of Crime, 1931.
70. DOOLEY, REV. EUGENE, O.M.I., J.C.L., Church Law on Sacred Relics, 1931.

www.ingramcontent.com/pod-product-compliance
Lightning Source LLC
LaVergne TN
LVHW050221080826
844660LV00012B/445
9780813222547